# Treasures of Jewish Heritage

## The Jewish Museum London

# Treasures of Jewish Heritage

## The Jewish Museum London

SCALA

This publication is dedicated to
Raymond Burton CBE and
Kenneth Rubens FRSA, OBE
in recognition of their outstanding contribution
to The Jewish Museum, London

# CONTRIBUTORS

**Dr David Bindman** is Durning-Lawrence Professor of History of Art at University College London, specialising in caricature and the history of printmaking, and in questions of national and racial identity. His most recent book is entitled *Ape to Apollo: Aesthetics and the Idea of Race in the 18th Century*.

**Rickie Burman** became Director of the Jewish Museum in 1995; she was previously Curator of the London Museum of Jewish Life, and also played a leading role in the establishment of the Manchester Jewish Museum. She trained as an anthropologist, and has published on the history of Jewish women in England, and on museology.

**Sir Martin Gilbert** is one of the foremost historians of the twentieth century. He has written more than 60 books, among them a definitive history of the Holocaust and a comprehensive study of the Second World War. Since 1962 he has been a Fellow of Merton College, Oxford (and an Honorary Fellow since 1994). He was knighted in 1995.

**Dr Anne J. Kershen** is founder/director of the Centre for the Study of Migration at Queen Mary, University of London. She studies the social, economic and political impact of immigration on East London. Her most recent book is *Strangers, Aliens and Asians*, a study of immigration to the Spitalfields district of London's East End.

**Jennifer Marin** was Education Officer and Assistant Curator of the Jewish Museum from 1988 until 1995, and has been Curator since 1995. She has curated numerous exhibitions, including *Angels and Demons: Jewish Magic and Mysticism*; *Judaica 2000: Contemporary Jewish Ceremonial Art*; and *Gibraltar Rock: British Fortress, Jewish Haven*.

**Anthony Phillips** is International Director of Silver and Objects of Vertu at Christie's. He is the co-author of *Antiquity Revisited*, a study of English Regency and French Napoleonic silver. He has been on the council of the Silver Society in London and is currently a member of the Antique Plate Committee of Goldsmiths' Hall.

**Dr Shalom Sabar** is Associate Professor of Jewish and Comparative Folklore at the Hebrew University of Jerusalem. Among his research interests are illuminated marriage contracts in Jewish communities around the world, and Jewish ceremonial and folk art, on which he has published widely.

**Lily Steadman** is Project Officer at the Jewish Museum. She studied psychology and philosophy at Oxford, and gained an MA in Gallery Studies at the University of Essex.

**Ilana Tahan** is Curator of the Hebrew Collections at the British Library, which range from centuries-old manuscripts and incunabula to the most recent printed materials. She has edited and compiled a number of publications relating to the Library's holdings, including a new collection of works by and relating to Maimonides.

**Jennifer Wearden** was, until her recent retirement, the Curator of Twentieth-Century European Textiles at the Victoria & Albert Museum. Her latest book is *Oriental Carpets and their Structure*, and she has published on a range of subjects, including samplers, Ottoman embroidery, Persian printed cottons and international costume.

# CONTENTS

# ACKNOWLEDGEMENTS

We are grateful for the support of the Museums, Libraries and Archives Council's Designation Challenge Fund, which has funded the production of digital photographs of the museum's Judaica collections and supported this publication. In addition, the following individuals and trusts have generously provided financial support, in honour of Raymond Burton and Kenneth Rubens, who have each played an invaluable role in the development of the Jewish Museum: Brenda and Anthony Abrahams, Ruth and Henry Amar, Edgar Astaire, Dr and Mrs Gerry Black, Sima and Ronald Channing, Anne Cowen and Michael Levenstein, Lynette and Robert Craig, Eva and Desmond Feldman, Jacqueline and Jonathan Gestetner, Dorothy and Michael Kauffmann, Avril Kleeman MBE, Colette and Peter Levy, Ruth and Brian Levy, Joanna Millan, Lord and Lady Moser, Sara Nathan, Sir Sigmund Sternberg KCSG and Lady Sternberg DOSS, the Wingate Charitable Trust, the Rt Hon. Lord Woolf and Lady Woolf.

The editorial team would like to thank all those who have contributed to the development of this publication and the collections it highlights. In particular, we would like to pay tribute to Edgar Samuel, Director of the Jewish Museum from 1981 until 1995, whose expertise and scholarship have helped to ensure the exceptional quality of its collections and who laid the foundations for its development as one of London's leading independent museums. We are also grateful to him for his input into the introductory chapter on the history of the museum.

Other colleagues who have assisted with the documentation and photography of the Museum's collections include: Carole Mendleson, former Curator; Alisa Jaffa, former Registrar; Louise Asher, Natinderjit Atwal and Darya Feuerstein, who assisted in the digitisation of the collections; Loveday Herridge and Carol Seigel, former Curators of the Jewish Museum, Finchley, and Sarah Jillings, who has played a key role both as present Curator of the Jewish Museum, Finchley and as Project Manager of the DCF project, which has made possible the production of this publication; and Museum Photographer Ian Lillicrapp, who, together with Jan Lawrie, photographed the entire Judaica collection and also undertook further photographic work in preparation for this publication. We acknowledge the contribution made by Carole Mendleson, Edgar Samuel and Carol Seigel to texts that have helped to shape the chapters on Jewish history in Britain and religious life.

Our thanks also go to all the authors who have contributed chapters on specific themes, and to the following for their help and comments: Edward van Voolen of the Jewish Historical Museum, Amsterdam; Felicitas Heimann-Jelinek of the Vienna Jewish Museum; Dr Grace Cohen Grossman of the Skirball Cultural Center, Los Angeles; and Professor Tony Kushner of the Parkes Institute, Southampton University.

Finally, we would like to record our gratitude to all our colleagues at the Jewish Museum, to Museum Chairman, Robert Craig, and to members of the Jewish Museum Council and Collections Committee.

**Rickie Burman, Jennifer Marin and Lily Steadman**

Supported by
MLA Designation
Challenge Fund

# FOREWORD

The Jewish Museum has long been close to my heart, and so I have been looking forward to this book – the first major publication of the collections since Richard Barnett's comprehensive 1974 catalogue, now out of print. The Museum is justifiably proud of having one of the world's finest collections of Jewish ceremonial art, rightly recognised as such through the award of Designated status by the Museums, Libraries and Archives Council.

This new book does full justice to the collections, with imaginative chapters on key media such as textiles and silver, and of course the Alfred Rubens collection of prints and drawings of Jewish life. These altogether remarkable collections are here lavishly illustrated with high-quality digital photographs, created with the support of the Designation Challenge Fund.

But what makes the book even more special is that it places these artistic wonders within the wider cultural context of Jewish, and indeed British, life and history. For example, as a Jewish refugee myself, I turned to Sir Martin Gilbert's chapter on refugees from Nazism. Naturally I found it authoritative as well as interesting. The chapters on Jewish history in Britain, the Jewish East End and the diverse roots of British Jews also offer informative background and showcase the Museum's social history collections.

And so, with wide-ranging chapters in the hands of leading scholars, we gain a picture of Jewish treasures and their relevance to our wider heritage.

I welcome this splendid book, a worthy tribute to the Museum and a fine way of marking the 350th anniversary of the readmission of Jews into Britain in 1656 – a landmark in the development of multicultural Britain. My congratulations to Rickie Burman, the Museum Director, and everyone else involved in this achievement.

Lord Moser KCB, CBE

# THE JEWISH MUSEUM, LONDON

## INTRODUCTION AND HISTORY

Rickie Burman

The Jewish Museum aims to explore Jewish heritage, celebrate diversity and challenge prejudice. It collects, preserves, interprets and exhibits material relating to Jewish history, culture and religious life, and draws on the Jewish experience as a focus for the exploration of identity in a multicultural society. As a forum for education, learning and inter-faith dialogue, the Museum encourages understanding and respect by challenging stereotypes and combating prejudice.

Since its establishment in 1932 the Jewish Museum has developed as one of London's leading independent museums, awarded Designated status by the Museums, Libraries and Archives Council in recognition of the outstanding national importance of its collections. With an acclaimed programme of education and exhibitions, it represents a major cultural and educational resource for London and the UK.

This publication highlights some of the treasures of the Museum but indicates too the range and diversity of its collections, and the experiences they represent. It builds on the precedent of the highly regarded *Catalogue of the Jewish Museum, London*, edited by R. D. Barnett (1974), combining essays by specialists in the field with photographs illustrating individual items; but its scope has been extended not only to include additional items acquired since the initial catalogue was produced but also to reflect some of the social history materials collected by the former London Museum of Jewish Life, which amalgamated with the Jewish Museum in 1995.

The history that follows traces the origins of the Jewish Museum, the later emergence of the London Museum of Jewish Life, and the subsequent development of the combined Museum. The latter brought together one of the world's finest collections of Jewish ceremonial art with a wide-ranging approach to Jewish social history, in order to explore the diverse heritage of Jewish people in Britain as one of the country's oldest minority communities.

# THE FIRST SIXTY YEARS

The founders of the Jewish Museum drew their inspiration and collections in part from the landmark *Anglo-Jewish Historical Exhibition,* held in 1887 at the Royal Albert Hall on the occasion of Queen Victoria's Jubilee. This exhibition placed on public view for the first time in Britain extensive collections of Jewish ritual art and aimed to counteract prejudice by disseminating information about the Jewish community and its contribution to English life. One of the principal organisers, Sir Isidore Spielmann, later commented: 'It showed to the outside world, which appeared to regard Jewish worship and all things Jewish as a kind of closed freemasonry or secret society, what Judaism really is and what the people really are. It … did something towards the education of our non-Jewish friends for the formation of a more correct estimate of us and our religion' (Presidential address to the Jewish Historical Society of England, 1903).

The Anglo-Jewish exhibition provided the impetus for the establishment in 1893 of the Jewish Historical Society of England, but while several museums of Jewish ritual art opened in continental Europe in the 1890s and during the first decade of the twentieth century, it was only in 1932 that the Jewish Museum in London was established. Before this date interest in England was still restricted to private collectors, foremost among them Arthur Franklin (1857–1938), brother-in-law of the first Lord Samuel, and Arthur Howitt (1885–1938), an early Zionist leader and Mayor of Richmond.

A combination of circumstances made possible the establishment of the Museum: the sale by Arthur Howitt of his Judaica collection and the development of a new Jewish Communal Centre at Woburn House, in Tavistock Square, Bloomsbury, to accommodate the United Synagogue, the Board of Deputies of British Jews and other institutions. The eminent historian Dr Cecil Roth had been engaged by Christie's to assist in preparing the catalogue for the Howitt collection and proposed to Sir Robert Waley Cohen, President of the

**JEWS' ORPHAN ASYLUM BANNER**
London, *c.*1831
Silk
1 m x 1 m
Bright blue silk banner with gold painted lettering.
The Jews' Orphan Asylum eventually merged with the Jews' Hospital to create the charity Norwood, which still works with Jewish families today.
1989.115

United Synagogue, the purchase of the collection in order to establish a Jewish Museum in the new centre. A friend of Roth and enthusiastic participant in founding the Museum was Wilfred Samuel (1887–1958), who helped to persuade Waley Cohen to accept the idea. The fledgling Museum accounted for almost one-third of the revenue from the sale of Howitt's collection.

The Jewish Museum opened to the public in April 1932, housed in the Library of the new Jews' College at Woburn House. Wilfred Samuel became the first Chairman of its Committee, and an energetic collector and fundraiser for the Museum. He recruited to the Committee a panel of experts to assess the quality of each object offered to the Museum. However, fundraising became more difficult with the growing need for charitable donations to help refugees from Nazi-occupied Europe. During the Second World War the Museum closed, and the collection was moved to a place of safety. Wilfred Samuel joined the forces and had a distinguished war record. Following the end of the war, the Museum was re-established in Jews' College Library.

Wilfred Samuel died in 1958, after twenty-six years as Chairman of the Jewish Museum Committee. He was succeeded by Alfred Rubens, who had joined as its expert on prints and drawings and continued as Chairman for the next twenty-five years. When Jews' College moved out of Woburn House into new premises in Montagu Place, the United Synagogue permitted the Museum to occupy the more spacious Rose Hertz Hall, where it reopened in June 1959.

In 1959 Wilfred Samuel's son Edgar Samuel was invited to join the Committee. A long-standing commitment to the Museum was evident too among some of the other families involved in its early development. The Museum's silver expert,

**GENERAL VIEW OF THE MUSEUM**
Charles Skilton & Fry Ltd, London, *c.*1960–80
Postcard
105 x 149 mm
The Jewish Museum at its previous location in Woburn House.

P. A. S. Phillips, was succeeded by his nephew Richard Norton and in turn by the latter's son Francis Norton. Furniture expert H. Blairman was succeeded by his son-in-law George Levy and then by his son Martin Levy.

Also in 1959 Alfred Rubens persuaded Dr Richard Barnett, Keeper of Western Asiatic Antiquities at the British Museum and Vice-Chairman of the Jewish Museum, to undertake the task of preparing a catalogue of the Museum's collection. When this was published by Harvey Miller in 1974, it set a new standard of excellence for Judaica catalogues. Alfred Rubens also engaged Carole Mendleson, a colleague of Richard Barnett's at the British Museum, for a day a week as the Museum's first professionally trained Curator. She improved standards of documentation and display, as well as producing an informative guidebook for visitors. Others who played a pivotal role were Sol Cohen, Secretary of the Jewish Memorial Council, and his successor, Phineas May, who later became a popular attendant at the Museum with the title of Honorary Custodian.

In 1982 Alfred Rubens announced his intention to retire from the Chair on reaching his eightieth birthday. The Committee agreed that the wide-ranging roles he had undertaken should now be divided between a Chairman, a Treasurer and a Director. Edgar Samuel agreed to serve as Director for an initial period of a year, a tenure which in fact lasted until 1995. He introduced audio-visual programmes explaining Judaism, increased the Museum's opening times to include weekdays as well as Sundays and further improved its documentation systems.

The chief long-term aim of both the Director and the Committee was now to move the Museum from Woburn House into its own premises. The existing accommodation had become cramped and inadequate for the Museum's needs, and plans to close Woburn House gave added urgency to this problem. The solution was reached when Raymond Burton, who had succeeded Richard Norton as Chairman, generously offered to donate and endow a new building for the Museum. He purchased two Grade II listed Victorian houses in Albert Street, Camden Town, then in use as an industrial workshop, and enlisted the help of Kenneth Rubens, nephew of Alfred Rubens, to manage the project of converting them to suit the Museum's requirements. Hunt Thompson Associates were appointed as architects, and exhibition designer Peter Ney was engaged to fit out the galleries, which were purpose-built in the garden area behind the original houses. In May 1995 HRH the Duke of Gloucester officially opened the Jewish Museum in its

**CEREMONIAL ART GALLERY**
© James Morris, London, 1994
The Ceremonial Art Gallery
of the Jewish Museum at its
location in Camden Town.

new premises, which at last provided an attractive and welcoming setting for its outstanding collection.

A further important development in 1995 was the amalgamation of the Jewish Museum with the former London Museum of Jewish Life, on a two-site basis. Following the opening, Edgar Samuel retired and was succeeded as Director by Rickie Burman, Curator of the London Museum of Jewish Life.

# CREATING THE MUSEUM COLLECTION

The Museum's early collecting policy aimed to illustrate Jewish religious practice and the history of the Jewish community in Britain with prints, portraits and ceremonial objects of historical interest and artistic merit. Initially acquisitions were limited to items over a hundred years old.

An important acquisition in 1932 was the fine seventeenth-century Italian synagogue ark, discovered at Chillingham Castle in Northumbria. Another major acquisition was the superb Judaica collection, loaned for display by Arthur Franklin and subsequently transferred to the Museum by Colin Franklin. An important priority was to rescue the silver, textiles and portraits of the City of London's three eighteenth-century Ashkenazi synagogues: the Great Synagogue, the New Synagogue and the Hambro. When the Hambro Synagogue closed in 1936, the United Synagogue made available its ceremonial textiles and objects. During the 1930s many such rare and important pieces were added to the collection, and the Museum's growing reputation led to an increase in the number of gifts and bequests.

The silver objects presented by the Spanish and Portuguese Jews' Congregation to the Lord Mayor of London between 1680 and 1780 were a particularly desirable addition. Another important group of acquisitions was a series of portraits donated by Alfred Rubens. In 1967 the Kahn Collection of synagogue textiles was purchased for the Museum. By 1974, when Barnett's *Catalogue of the Jewish Museum* was published, the Museum had built up a collection of Jewish ceremonial objects of world importance, as well as a fine collection of portraits, medallions, prints and documents illustrating Jewish history in eighteenth- and nineteenth-century Britain.

In 1983 the United Synagogue deposited a number of important paintings in the Museum, including portraits of past Chief Rabbis. Ten years later, when the United Synagogue decided to sell some remarkable silver pieces from the former Great Synagogue, the Museum was able to step in and purchase some of the finest items including the unique silver Torah scrolls made for the *Ba'al Shem* of London, Rabbi Falk.

Following the relocation of the Museum to its new premises in Camden Town, Alfred Rubens loaned and subsequently bequeathed his outstanding collection of prints and drawings. A further major acquisition took place in 1998 with the transfer

*Above:*
**MEDALLION**
Byzantium, sixth to eighth century
Gold
65 mm diameter
Disc, possibly for ornamenting a scroll of the Law. Decorated with Jewish symbols, including *menorah, shofar* and *lulav,* and bearing an inscription in Greek: 'For the vow of Jacob, the leader, the pearl-seller.' One of the Museum's earliest acquisitions.
JM 2

*Opposite:*
**TORAH CROWN**
Galicia or Hungary, early nineteenth century
Silver-gilt
285 mm high, 130 mm diameter (at base)
Base ring with pierced applied bands of foliage supporting six lions rampant, with bells between; a further band of foliage supports six stags upholding a basket, with a vine spray or blackberry finial. Acquired by the Jewish Museum as part of the Gustave Tuck collection.
C 2001.5.5

of part of the Gustave Tuck Collection of ceremonial objects to the Museum by the Jewish Historical Society of England. The collection has continued to develop in size and quality. One of the Museum's current priorities is to reflect and encourage the growing interest in contemporary Judaica, especially among British artists and designers. Following the Museum's exhibition *Judaica 2000*, a *kiddush* cup by Gerald Benney and an *etrog* container by Mila Tanya Griebel were acquired.

In 1997 the Jewish Museum was awarded Designated status by the Museums and Galleries Commission (now the Museums, Libraries and Archives Council) in recognition of the outstanding importance of its Judaica collections as part of the national heritage.

# THE LONDON MUSEUM OF JEWISH LIFE, 1983–95

The amalgamation of the Jewish Museum with the London Museum of Jewish Life in 1995 brought together two museums with contrasting collections and approaches to Jewish history.

Like many Jewish people in Britain, the London Museum of Jewish Life had its roots in the East End of London. It was founded in 1983, initially with the title the Museum of the Jewish East End, as a result of concern that material relating to this heartland of Jewish settlement was disappearing, and that no record would be left of the Jewish immigrant experience and the vibrant Jewish life that had once flourished in the area.

The Museum grew out of the Jewish East End Project (JEEP), initiated under the auspices of the Association for Jewish Youth with inspiration from the East End historian William Fishman. Enthusiasts David Jacobs, Harriet Karsh and Monty Richardson, who were all involved in Jewish youth and community work, together with others, including Gerry Black and Derek Reid, organised a number of ground-breaking events in the Stepney Jewish Settlement, one of the last surviving Jewish institutions in the East End. A Jewish East End Festival in 1980 was followed by a major conference on 'The Jewish East End: 1840–1939', held in conjunction with the Jewish Historical Society. The success of both events demonstrated the wide interest in learning about the Jewish East End and the experiences of the Jewish immigrants from Eastern Europe who had made it their home.

Although JEEP could not continue, since the Association for Jewish Youth was unable to maintain its co-ordinating role, several associated individuals became actively involved in the establishment of the Museum of the Jewish East End and served on its initial committee. It had now become apparent that there was an urgent need to preserve and house material reflecting immigrant life, especially since the acquisition policy of the older-established Jewish Museum excluded materials less than a hundred years old.

Just as in the 1930s the development of a new communal centre in Woburn House had facilitated the founding of the Jewish Museum, so in the 1980s the development of the Museum of the Jewish East End was made possible by the establishment of the Manor House Centre for Judaism (later the Sternberg Centre for Judaism) in an eighteenth-century manor house in Finchley, a suburb of North London. The director of the new centre, Rabbi Tony Bayfield, gave his active support to the project and in 1983 provided accommodation for the nascent Museum, at the suggestion of William Fishman and David Jacobs. In a further parallel, while the Jewish Museum was founded in premises associated with the United Synagogue and Jews' College, an Orthodox rabbinical college, the new Museum was initiated in a communal centre developed by the Reform Synagogues of Great Britain, Leo Baeck College (a rabbinical college for the Reform and Liberal movements) and a Masorti congregation, the New North London Synagogue. In each case, although nurtured by a particular religious movement, the Museum was established as an independent registered charity. Both museums were also among the first in the UK to achieve registered status.

The Museum's early development was greatly assisted by a grant awarded in 1984 by the Greater London Council to employ a full-time Curator. The Museum Committee appointed to the post Rickie Burman, who had played a lead role in establishing the Manchester Jewish Museum, as Project Co-ordinator and Research Fellow in the pioneering Jewish History Unit established by historian Bill Williams at the Manchester Studies Unit. Following the opening of the Manchester Jewish Museum in 1984, she moved to London to take up the new challenge of developing the Museum of the Jewish East End. In doing so, she drew on her experience in recovering and recording Jewish heritage in Manchester, and a background in anthropology and oral history. A grant secured from the government's Manpower Services Commission enabled the Museum to employ young graduates on a temporary basis between 1985 and 1988, providing an important foundation for the development of the Museum and its collections.

In 1985 Robert Craig succeeded Rabbi Bayfield as Chairman of the Museum Committee. From the outset the Museum of the Jewish East End sought to complement the collections of the existing Jewish Museum by a more inclusive approach that encompassed objects reflecting everyday life and a wide range of social history materials. It started to collect materials relating to working life, such as tailoring, cabinetmaking and furriers' tools, items relating to life in the home, political activity and the many synagogues, clubs and institutions that served the immigrant population in the East End. An active approach to collecting was adopted; when the last Jewish bakery in the East End closed down, the Museum managed to retrieve its dough trough and baking implements; similarly, material from the Jewish Soup Kitchen and the Workers' Circle, a socialist Jewish friendly society, was collected as these institutions

other experiences that also needed to be recovered to reflect the diversity of Jewish roots and life in Britain, and in 1988 it changed its name to the London Museum of Jewish Life. Exhibitions followed on the experience of refugees from Nazism and Holocaust survivors, *Living Up West* on the Jews of the West End, a special exhibition on the Jews of Aden, and

ceased to operate. In addition to acquiring objects and documents, the Museum established Photographic and Oral History Archives, which continue to form an important part of its collections today.

The exhibitions mounted by the Museum in its early years gave recognition for the first time to the experiences of the immigrant generation and their children, in the words of one visitor 'bringing back many memories and many heartaches'. At the same time they served an important role in augmenting its collections. An exhibition marking the centenary of the Jews' Temporary Shelter was followed by *A Century of Migration*, providing an overview of the Jewish East End experience and the foundation for the Museum's permanent displays. A highly successful exhibition featured Boris Bennett, the legendary East End wedding photographer. As part of the Jewish East End Celebration in 1987, the Museum mounted *East End Synagogues*, marking the centenary of the Federation of Synagogues, in the atmospheric setting of the former Princelet Street synagogue, and a major exhibition on *Yiddish Theatre in London* at the National Theatre on London's South Bank. Another exhibition, *Off-the-Peg*, curated by historian Anne Kershen, looked at the Jewish role in the development of the women's ready-to-wear garment industry.

As the Museum progressed, it was recognised that, while the East End was a crucial part of Jewish history, there were

*A Tapestry of Many Threads*, on the experience of Jewish immigrants who had settled in Britain from areas as diverse as Iraq, Iran, Morocco, Tunisia, Egypt and India.

In each case the exhibition served as a focus for collecting, as well as for the recognition of the diverse groups and experiences represented amongst the Jewish community. At the same time these exhibitions performed an important role in breaking down stereotypes, demonstrating to the wider community the heterogeneity of Jewish people and their roots, and communicating commonalities of working life, political life, social activities and human values. Jewish experience was thus presented as an integral part of British society and history.

Alongside its exhibition programme the Museum also developed a highly regarded programme of education. Activities included drama workshops and programmes exploring Jewish roots, and the Museum gained increasing recognition for its pioneering work in Holocaust and anti-racist education. In addition, several of the initiatives developed by JEEP were maintained: a programme of guided walks round the Jewish East End, extended to include walking tours of the Jewish City of London; talks, lectures and a Research Group to encourage interest among both academics and laypeople; and a Family History Workshop, which was later to evolve into the Jewish Genealogical Society of Great Britain. It also undertook outreach work, with off-site talks and travelling displays.

# DEVELOPMENTS SINCE 1995

The amalgamation of the Jewish Museum with the London Museum of Jewish Life in 1995 brought the two museums together under a single management. Although, as a result of space constraints, it was not possible at that stage to combine on one site, a single board of trustees was formed, with membership drawn from the two previous boards. Kenneth Rubens continued as Chairman of the merged Jewish Museum, while Robert Craig, the former Chairman of the London Museum of Jewish Life, served as Deputy Chairman, succeeding Kenneth Rubens as Chairman in 2004.

The Jewish Museum continued to operate two museum sites with complementary collections, activities and displays. At its Camden Town location the Museum housed a Ceremonial Art Gallery, a History Gallery providing an overview of British Jewish history, and a temporary exhibitions gallery; while at the Jewish Museum, Finchley displays focused on Jewish social history and the experience of immigration and settlement in London, with reconstructions of tailoring and cabinetmaking workshops.

In 1996 a Holocaust Education Gallery was established at the Museum's Finchley location, with a poignant display focusing on the experiences of Leon Greenman OBE, an Auschwitz survivor, born in London's East End. The Museum's Holocaust and anti-racist education programmes provided young people with the opportunity to meet a survivor and to ask questions and engage in discussion. At Camden Town, *Discovering Judaism* programmes were developed to offer a hands-on, creative approach to learning.

In 1997 the Rt Hon. Chris Smith, Secretary of State for Culture, visited the Museum to present its award of Designated status. The Museum was also highly commended as Visitor Attraction of the Year in the London Tourism Awards 2000. Grant awards from the Designation Challenge Fund enabled the Museum to create digital photographs of its outstanding collections, to transfer data about the collections to a computer-based management system and provide access through a web-based on-line catalogue and other media. In addition, the Museum participated as a Senior Partner in the prestigious *Moving Here* project, contributing some 15,000 images to a website on migration to England, created by a consortium of museums, libraries and archives, led by the National Archives.

**EDUCATION PROGRAMME
WITH HOLOCAUST SURVIVOR
LEON GREENMAN OBE**
Ian Lillicrapp, London, *c.*1998

In forging the combined Jewish Museum, the aim has been to build on the strengths of both constituent museums. In our exhibition programme since amalgamation we have sought to achieve a synthesis of the approaches of both museums: to integrate the display of art-historical and social history materials, and to bring together artefacts with the stories and life experiences of the individuals who used or created them. The Museum has continued to develop ground-breaking exhibitions on a wide range of themes, and at the same time has gained recognition as a venue for high-profile international exhibitions. Notable exhibitions have included *Coats of Many Colours: Jewish Costume and Customs around the World*; *Angels and Demons: Jewish Magic and Mysticism*; *Continental Britons: Jewish Refugees from Nazi Europe*; *By the Rivers of Babylon: The Story of the Jews of Iraq*; *A Time to be Born: Beginning Life in Jewish Tradition*; *Gibraltar Rock: British Fortress, Jewish Haven*; and *Closing the Door? Immigrants to Britain 1905–2005*, an influential exhibition marking the centenary of the 1905 Aliens Act.

The Museum has continued its outreach programme, with travelling displays touring all over Britain to venues ranging from schools and libraries to museums, galleries and even cathedrals. Examples include *The Boys*, the story of 732 teenage Holocaust survivors admitted to Britain after the Second World War, and an exhibition on the Kindertransport, *The Last Goodbye: The Rescue of Children from Nazi Europe*, accompanied by an associated education resource. The Museum's exhibitions have been shown all over Britain, from Pontypridd to Invergordon, as well as internationally.

Following the amalgamation, it became a priority for the trustees to expand the Museum at its flagship premises in Camden Town and to integrate all its collections and activities within a single site. The first step was achieved with the acquisition of a four-storey former piano factory adjoining the rear of the Museum's Albert Street premises, with the generous assistance of Raymond Burton, Kenneth Rubens and other donors. In 2005 the Jewish Museum Development Project was established to raise funds for its expansion, which would triple the size of the Camden Town site and provide much-needed additional accommodation for enlarged exhibition galleries, improved visitor services and educational facilities, including an auditorium and education centre.

The many messages of support received for the Development Project highlighted the Museum's achievement, both in preserving and exploring the diverse roots and heritage of Jewish people as one of Britain's oldest minorities, and in contributing to contemporary life through a positive recognition of diversity, building connections, understanding and respect.

'In a society such as ours where multiculturalism has and will continue to play an inestimable role creatively and culturally, the Jewish Museum is of national importance.' The Rt Hon. Glenda Jackson MP

'The stories you tell are the stories London needs to hear; they are the stories of all our pasts and essential for underscoring our collective identity.' Professor Jack Lohman, Director, Museum of London

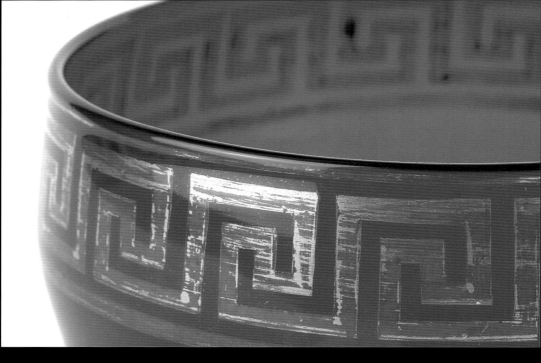

# JEWISH HISTORY IN BRITAIN

The story of the Jewish community in Britain begins with
an initial settlement in the medieval period, terminated
by the expulsion of the Jews in 1290. For more than
350 years there was no formal Jewish presence in this
country. Following the Readmission under Oliver Cromwell
in 1656, Jewish people have lived and worshipped
openly in Britain.

# THE MEDIEVAL JEWISH COMMUNITY

Jewish people were first recorded as settling in Britain at the time of the Norman Conquest in 1066, when William the Conqueror encouraged the Jewish population of Rouen, the capital city of Normandy, to come to England in order to stimulate the economy. However, during the medieval period Christian guilds gradually developed control over trades and crafts. Jews were increasingly forced into usury, which the Church banned Christians from undertaking. The Jewish community faced heavy taxes but still prospered and made contributions to Talmudic scholarship.

In the twelfth century the preaching of the Crusades against the 'Infidel' led to attacks on Jews in most Western countries. In 1189 King Richard I refused to receive Jewish delegates to his coronation. This sign of hostility led to brutal attacks on Jewish quarters in London and other cities. Amongst the worst of these was the siege of Clifford's Tower in York, where the Jewish community had taken refuge from their attackers; rather than fall into the hands of the mob, they committed mass suicide. Persecution worsened under Edward I and finally, in 1290, an Edict of Expulsion was issued, ordering all Jews to leave England. This was part of a pattern of similar expulsions taking place throughout Europe during the Middle Ages.

From 1290 until 1656 there was officially no Jewish community in England. However, a number of 'secret Jews' fled from Spain and Portugal during this period in order to

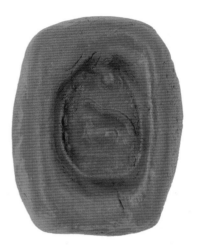

**SIGNET RING AND IMPRESSION**
Thirteenth century, said to have been found in Kent in 1929
Brass
16 x 22 mm
Bezel engraved with design of snake and ram and inscribed in Hebrew with the name Aaron.
JM 1202

escape persecution, forced baptism and the Inquisition. Some of these Sephardi Jews came to England, where they worshipped outwardly as Christians but continued to practise Judaism in private. One such was Dr Rodrigo Lopez, who for a time served as physician to Queen Elizabeth I, until he was accused of plotting her death and was executed as a traitor in 1594.

**PAIR OF TALLY STICKS**
Gloucester, thirteenth century
Wood
180 mm long
These tallies were given as receipts – notches were made to indicate the sum received, and the tallies were then split down the centre, each half acting as a confirmation of the other.
(*Top*) Tally inscribed and notched for a payment of £84 13s 4d.
JM 653a
(*Bottom*) Tally inscribed in ink, indicating a payment of one shilling by Isaac (the Gloucester *shochet*, or ritual butcher) on account of a tallage of 20,000 marks.
JM 653

# The Readmission

In 1655 Rabbi Menasseh ben Israel, of Amsterdam, published a pamphlet called *The Hope of Israel*. In this he used biblical texts to argue that, in order for the Messianic age to come, there must be Jews in all parts of the world, including England. Menasseh travelled here to petition Oliver Cromwell, the Lord Protector, on this matter. Cromwell may have been influenced by Menasseh's arguments; he was certainly in favour of religious toleration and aware of the economic benefits the return of Jewish people would bring, thanks to their access to wide trading networks – the Netherlands were already benefiting from such links, owing to the settlement of large numbers of Spanish and Portuguese Jews in Amsterdam. In 1656 it was at last ruled that the Edict of Expulsion had only applied to Jews living in England in 1290; after nearly 400 years of exile Jewish people could therefore return to England and were allowed to 'meet privately in their houses for prayer'.

**PORTRAIT OF A MAN BELIEVED
TO BE MENASSEH BEN ISRAEL**
Seventeenth century
Etching from an original
by Rembrandt, second state
108 x 108 mm
AR 1806

# THE EARLY SEPHARDI COMMUNITY

The newly formed Sephardi Jewish community founded a synagogue at Creechurch Lane in the City of London, and a burial ground was leased at Mile End, further to the east. In 1701 Bevis Marks, a new larger synagogue with seats for 400 men and 160 women, was constructed near the old one; it continues in use as the oldest active synagogue in Britain.

During the eighteenth century the Sephardi community in Britain flourished. Immigrants arrived from across southern Europe, and they largely prospered, many working as physicians, jewellers, engravers, confectioners or street traders. One of the most successful was Samson Gideon, who became a wealthy financier and was often called upon to underwrite government debts. The most famous eighteenth-century Jewish Briton was Daniel Mendoza, a popular hero and champion boxer of England for most years between 1788 and 1795. He introduced a new 'scientific' style of boxing and was the first boxer to receive royal patronage. Always billed as 'Mendoza the Jew', he did much to raise the positive profile of Jewish people among the general public.

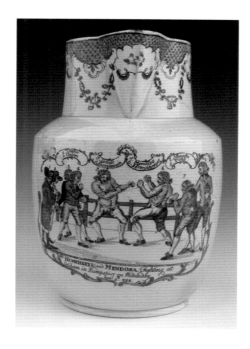

*Left:*
**DANIEL MENDOZA JUG**
John Aynsley, Stoke-on-Trent, *c.*1800
Ceramic
127 mm high
Jug depicting Richard Humphries and Daniel Mendoza 'Fighting at Odiham in Hampshire on Wednesday 9 January 1788'.
JM 686

*Right:*
**INTERIOR OF THE SPANISH AND PORTUGUESE SYNAGOGUE (BEVIS MARKS), LONDON**
By D. Havell, from an engraving by Isaac Mendes Belisario, 1817
Aquatint
319 x 433 mm
C 1988.54

# THE EARLY ASHKENAZI COMMUNITY

Meanwhile, a community from a different background had begun to arrive in Britain. The Ashkenazim came mostly from Germany, and later from Poland and Russia. There were great extremes of wealth and poverty among the new arrivals. One of the wealthiest was Nathan Mayer Rothschild (1777–1836), founder of one of the world's greatest banking empires. Others were exceedingly poor and scratched a living selling ribbons, watches, jewellery or old clothes. The Jewish pedlar became a familiar figure throughout the country.

*Above:*
**A VIEW FROM THE ROYAL EXCHANGE**
Printed by E. Ronicke, Leipzig, nineteenth century (possibly from an original by Richard Dighton)
Lithograph
215 x 184 mm
Profile of Nathan Mayer Rothschild
AR 2132

*Right:*
**JEWISH PEDLAR**
Rockingham, *c.*1820
Porcelain
130 mm high
Figurine of Jewish old clothes man, holding two hats, one black and one white, and with a brown sack over his shoulder.
JM 694

*Opposite:*
**PAIR OF PEDLARS**
Royal Crown Derby, Derby, *c.*1760
Porcelain
Female figure 287 mm high; male figure 280 mm high
Pair of Derby ware figures of two Jewish pedlars, possibly husband and wife. The woman carries a box of trinkets in one hand and ribbons in the other, while the man carries bottles.
JM 693a

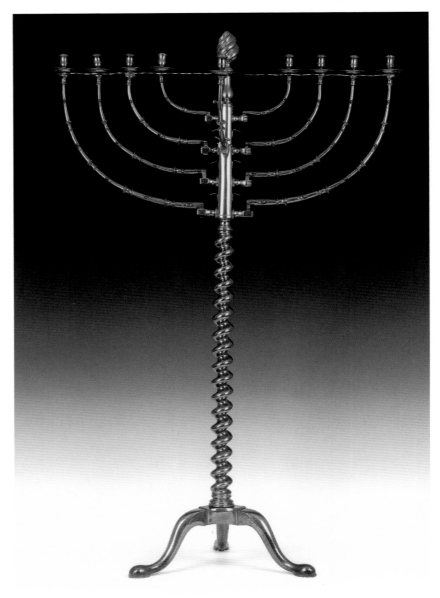

*Left:*
**NEW SYNAGOGUE TABLE-TOP**
England, *c.*1850
Papier mâché
813 x 588 mm
Round-topped table decorated with a picture of the New Synagogue at the festival of *Sukkot*. At the Great Exhibition in 1851 similar papier mâché tables were exhibited, with pictures of Windsor and Winchester castles.
JM 12

*Right:*
*HANUKAH* LAMP
England, early eighteenth century
Brass
1.89 x 1.22 m
Standing candelabrum from the Hambro Synagogue, on tripod club feet, with spiral stem. Eight curved branches spring from hands, with writhen finial and beadle light.
JM 234

The first Ashkenazi synagogue, the Great Synagogue, was founded in 1692 in Duke's Place in the City of London, and two further major synagogues, the Hambro and the New, opened in the next seventy years. These three synagogues were the original constituents of the modern United Synagogue.

During the eighteenth century the Jewish population of Britain increased to 30,000, and synagogues were founded in many provincial towns. Wars with France and the expansion of the Royal Navy enabled Jewish dealers in marine supplies and optical instruments to become established in West Country seaports. The Board of Deputies of British Jews, founded in 1760, represented the whole community on political and legal matters.

By the start of the nineteenth century the community's
leaders were increasingly drawn from the Ashkenazim,
generally from a handful of influential families. Whilst
considerable variations in wealth and status remained, the
community was gradually becoming more prosperous, better
educated and more integrated into British life. One particularly
important figure in the community at this time was Sir Moses
Montefiore (1784–1885), a successful businessman who was
able to retire at the age of forty and devote himself to
charitable and diplomatic work on behalf of Jewish people in
Britain and across the world. In 1817 the Jews' Free School
was opened and an apprenticeship scheme set up. In 1840 the
West London Synagogue was founded, reflecting a desire by
some Jews to move to a form of worship more in keeping with
the customs of the country in which they now lived; similar
moves toward liberalisation were also being made in Central
Europe. This marked the start of Reform Judaism, a movement
that gained further support in the twentieth century.

**BOYS LEARNING TO LAY THE PHYLACTERIES**
London, 1908
Mounted photograph
600 x 800 mm
Boys at the Jews' Free School learning how to put on *tefillin*.
E 1991.240

Left:
**REPULSED BUT NOT DISCOURAGED**
Published by Thomas McLean, England, 1830
Lithograph
266 x 368 mm
Satirical print showing a Jew attempting to enter Parliament. In the centre stands Daniel O'Connell, leader of the Catholic emancipation movement, saying: 'Agitate, friend Moses, Agitate! That's the way I got in.'
AR 996

Below:
**SIR DAVID SALOMONS**
Solomon Alexander Hart, RA, London, c.1856
Oil on canvas
1.11 x 0.90 m
Portrait of Sir David Salomons in his robes as Lord Mayor of London. On loan from Guildhall Art Gallery. Image courtesy of Guildhall Library, Corporation of London.
E 258

# EMANCIPATION

Since the English Civil War political debate in Britain had focused on whether those who were not members of the Church of England could hold positions of authority in the state.

Anyone born overseas could only be naturalised as a British citizen if they took the sacrament according to the Church of England. In 1753 an Act of Parliament, popularly known as the 'Jew Bill', enabled Jewish immigrants to be naturalised, but it had to be repealed after a popular outcry. It was not until 1835 that the naturalisation of Jewish people was finally permitted. Other restrictions were also lifted in the mid-nineteenth century; for example, Jews were admitted to municipal office in 1845, and allowed to take degrees at Cambridge University in 1856, and at Oxford in 1871.

David Salomons (1797–1873) was elected Sheriff of the City of London in 1835 and went on to become the first Jewish Lord Mayor. In 1847 Lionel de Rothschild was elected MP for the City of London, but he was unable to take his seat as he would not make his statutory declaration 'on the true faith of a Christian'. David Salomons was also returned to Parliament in 1851, facing the same restriction. It was not until 1858, after Rothschild had won four successive election victories, that the oath was amended, finally allowing him to become the first practising Jew to serve as a Member of Parliament.

*Left:*
**THE LAW**
Sir Leslie Ward ('Spy'), London,
1 March 1879
Chromolithograph
310 x 184 mm
*Vanity Fair* caricature of Sir
George Jessel, from the 'Men of
the Day' series.
AR 1703

The first Jew to hold ministerial office was George Jessel, who was made Solicitor-General in 1871; he later became Master of the Rolls. By the end of the century Nathaniel de Rothschild had been appointed to the peerage, and in 1908 Herbert Samuel joined the Cabinet. Rufus Isaacs was appointed Lord Chief Justice in 1913 and later became Viceroy of India.

*Right:*
**RUFUS**
Sir Leslie Ward ('Spy'), London,
18 February 1904
Chromolithograph
295 x 192 mm
*Vanity Fair* caricature of Rufus
Isaacs, 1st Viscount Reading.
AR 1673

*Above:*

**SALOMONS CARRIAGE DOORS**

England, nineteenth century
Leather, wood, gilt
407 x 369 mm
Pair of carriage doors decorated
with the coat of arms of Sir
David Salomons.
C 1976.1.13.2

*Below:*

***HANUKAH* LAMP MADE FROM
A SHELL CASE**

Palestine, 1920s
Brass
113 x 281 x 130 mm
Lamp presented to Herbert Samuel in
his capacity as High Commissioner for Palestine (1920–25).
Engraved with arcading containing hanging lamps and
Hebrew inscriptions including prayers for *Hanukah* and a
dedication to Samuel.
JM 273

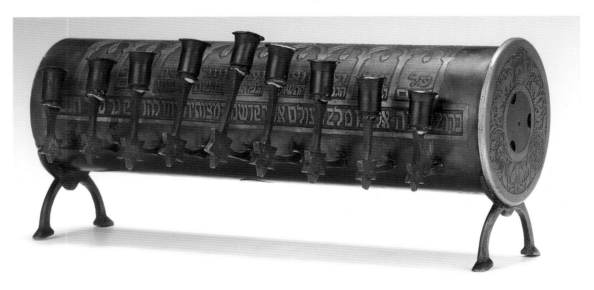

# THE GREAT MIGRATION

During the second half of the nineteenth century the Jewish population of Eastern Europe was facing increased economic hardship and persecution. Jewish residence in Russia was confined to the Pale of Settlement, and permitted occupations were restricted. Following the assassination of Tsar Alexander II in 1881, the situation worsened. Jewish communities were subject to widespread pogroms – violent mass attacks, often officially instigated.

**MIZRACH**

Annie Grossman, Russia, *c.*1896
Paper, wool, cotton, beads
444 x 542 mm
Hand-embroidered *mizrach* with symmetrical motifs including birds, candles, ladders and Hebrew characters. This was made by Annie Grossman in Russia, and brought to England on the occasion of her marriage to Max Grossman, who had already made the same journey.
1986.135.1

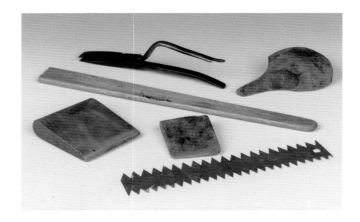

Between 1881 and 1914 over 2 million Jewish people left Russia and Poland. While the majority went to the United States, around 150,000 settled in Britain, often in areas near the docks where they had arrived, in the East End of London and in provincial centres such as Manchester, Leeds, Liverpool and Glasgow. Here they found employment in low-wage, labour-intensive industries, and their presence had a dramatic impact on the Jewish community in Britain. Among the immigrants was Michael Marks, who started his career on a street stall and went on to found Marks and Spencer.

As new immigrants arrived, conditions in the East End became increasingly difficult and overcrowded. In response, the established Jewish community set up many charities to assist those in need. Notable institutions included the Jewish Board of Guardians, the orphanage which later moved to Norwood, and the Jews' Temporary Shelter, giving short-term assistance to new arrivals.

The new immigrants generated a distinctive and vibrant culture. Numerous small synagogues, *hevrot*, were founded in all types of premises. While the children learned English in school, many of the adult immigrants continued to speak their native Yiddish, a language derived from Hebrew and German; Yiddish newspapers and literature were widely available, and Yiddish theatre flourished. However, the large numbers of Jewish people arriving in Britain aroused hostility, and calls to curb immigration came from some quarters. In 1905 the Aliens Act was passed in order to restrict Jewish entry to Britain, and the outbreak of the First World War in 1914 brought immigration to a halt.

# BRITISH JEWRY AND ZIONISM

In reaction to the international events of this period the Zionist movement began to develop. The Zionist ideal of creating a modern Jewish state initially received mixed reactions from the Anglo-Jewish community – despite sympathy for the plight of Eastern European Jews, there was a fear that the assertion of a separate Jewish nationality might undermine their hard-won status as British citizens. This began to change in 1895 and 1896, when Theodor Herzl visited Britain to promote the arguments contained in his book *The Jewish State*. His ideas took root, and in 1899 the English Zionist Federation was founded.

Among the most prominent British Zionists was the writer Israel Zangwill (1864–1926), who was also an active campaigner for causes such as pacifism and women's suffrage. He was born to poor immigrant parents from Russia and Poland, and was educated at the Jews' Free School, where he began his career as a teacher. Zangwill founded the Jewish Territorialist Organization, whose goal was to obtain territory – not necessarily in Palestine – for Jewish settlement.

"I am a Jew, of course I am proud of it. The advantage of being of Jewish birth, brought me into relation with a good deal of suffering all over the world, and I appreciate more than Englishmen possibly may do the great advantage the English enjoy in the possession of liberty in their constitution."
Israel Zangwill

Theodor Herzl died in 1904, the same year that Chaim Weizmann, a young Russian scientist, settled in Manchester. Later to become the first President of the State of Israel, Weizmann spearheaded the movement to achieve official British recognition of the Zionist cause. In November 1917 the Balfour Declaration was issued, pledging the British government's support for 'the establishment in Palestine of a national home for the Jewish people'. This was given a more concrete basis at the end of the First World War, when Palestine, as a part of the former Ottoman Empire, was placed under British mandate. However, it was not until after the Second World War, partly in response to the Holocaust, that the creation of an autonomous Jewish state received general support. In 1948 the British government withdrew from Mandate Palestine, and the State of Israel was proclaimed. British Jews were to have a significant role in supporting the State of Israel and, for many, Zionism became an important facet of their Jewish identity.

# Taking Refuge in Britain

In the 1930s a new wave of immigrants arrived in Britain, fleeing from Germany and other countries under Nazi control. In 1933 the Nazi party under Adolf Hitler had come to power in Germany, with an openly anti-Semitic policy. The Nazi government encouraged violence against Jewish people and their homes and property, and removed their civil rights. Fearing for their lives, many German Jews sought to emigrate, but few countries were prepared to receive them.

The British Union of Fascists (BUF) was active from 1932, engaging in acts of violence against Jewish people and buildings, particularly in the East End of London. This culminated with Oswald Mosley and his 'blackshirts' attempting to march through East London on 4 October 1936. Under the slogan 'They Shall Not Pass', a crowd estimated at 10,000, including Communist and Labour groups, such as dockers, as well as Jews, turned out to block the streets; the resultant violent clashes became known as the 'Battle of Cable Street'. Fascism never took root in Britain, and the BUF was disbanded in 1940.

About 60,000 Jewish refugees were able to come to Britain before war broke out. Many were highly educated, from professional or artistic backgrounds. However, in order to be admitted to Britain, they had to find jobs before leaving Germany; in their search for safety they often took positions as domestic servants. About 10,000 unaccompanied children came on the Kindertransport, many destined never to see their parents again.

**WHILE YOU ARE IN ENGLAND**
German Jewish Aid Committee & Board of Deputies of British Jews London, *c.*1933–39
Card, paper
153 x 90 mm
From a booklet of 'helpful information and guidance for every refugee', in German and English. Includes advice on appropriate behaviour, such as speaking English at all times when in public, never criticising the government, and not dressing in a conspicuous manner.
1988.488.1

1. Spend your spare time immediately in learning the English language and its correct pronunciation.

2. Refrain from speaking German in the streets and in public conveyances and in public places such as restaurants. Talk halting English rather than fluent German— and *do not talk in a loud voice*. Do not read German newspapers in public.

3. Do not criticise any Government regulations, nor the way things are done over here. Do not speak of "how much better this or that is done in Germany". It may be true in some matters, but it weighs as nothing against the sympathy and freedom and liberty of England which are now given to you. Never forget that point.

4. Do not join any Political organisation, or take part in any political activities.

5. Do not make yourself conspicuous by speaking loudly, nor by your manner or dress. The Englishman greatly dislikes ostentation, loudness of dress or manner, or unconventionality of dress or manner. The Englishman attaches very great importance to modesty, under-statement in speech rather than over-statement, and quietness of dress and manner. He values good manners far more than he values the

*Page 12*

**Betrachten Sie sie bitte als Ehrenpflichten :**

1. Verwenden Sie Ihre freie Zeit unverzüglich zur Erlernung der englischen Sprache und ihrer richtigen Aussprache.

2. Sprechen Sie nicht deutsch in den Strassen, in Verkehrsmitteln oder sonst in der Öffentlichkeit, wie z.B. in Restaurants. Sprechen Sie lieber stockend englisch als fliessend deutsch—und sprechen Sie nicht laut. Lesen Sie keine deutschen Zeitungen in der Öffentlichkeit.

3. Kritisieren Sie weder Bestimmungen der Regierung noch irgendwelche englischen Gebräuche. Sprechen Sie nicht davon, "um wieviel besser dies oder das in Deutschland getan wird". Es mag manchmal wahr sein, aber es bedeutet nichts gegenüber der Sympathie und Freiheit Englands, die Ihnen jetzt gewährt werden. Vergessen Sie diesen Punkt niemals.

4. Treten Sie weder einer politischen Organisation bei, noch nehmen Sie sonst Anteil an politischen Bewegungen.

5. Benehmen Sie sich nicht auffallend durch lautes Sprechen, durch Ihre Manieren oder Kleidung. Dem Engländer missfallen Schaustellungen, auffallende oder nicht-konventionelle Kleidung und Manieren.

*Seite 13*

At the start of the Second World War many of these recent refugees were interned as enemy aliens. Following public protest most were released by late 1940, and many of them joined the Pioneer Corps and fought courageously for the British armed forces. They also contributed to the war effort in other ways, on the home front and later as camp liberators and relief workers.

Some survivors of Nazi concentration camps were allowed to settle in Britain. In 1946 the British government agreed to admit 1,000 young survivors of the camps, but only 732 could be found. This group of teenage survivors became known as 'the Boys', although some were actually girls. Through their comradeship they helped each other to build new lives.

These refugees from Nazism have added a further dimension to the experience of Jewish people in Britain, and many have had a significant impact on British life.

*Above:*
**JOHNNY BLUNT AND COMRADES
IN THE PIONEER CORPS**
Brussels, 1944
Photograph
140 x 65 mm
Johnny Blunt, seen here
bayoneting a swastika, was born
in Germany. He came to
England as a child refugee on
the Kindertransport in
December 1938 and later joined
the Pioneer Corps to fight
Nazism in Europe.
608.17

# JEWISH LIFE IN MODERN BRITAIN

Since the Second World War the Jewish community in Britain has continued to develop in many different ways. Today very few Jewish people live in the East End of London or in the early heartlands of Jewish settlement in other British cities. In London the move to the suburbs began prior to the First World War and accelerated with the extension of the Underground system and the development of suburban housing; it was also strongly affected by the Blitz.

By the 1920s and 1930s Jewish communities had been established in areas such as Golders Green, Edgware and Ilford, and today there are thriving communities in outer London

*Above:*
**MIRIAM SOLOMON WITH
HER SON SAMMY**
India, *c.*1890
Photograph
The Solomon family, whose Indian name
was Dhigorker, left India to settle in
Britain during the twentieth century.
1115.4

suburbs such as Radlett and Bushey. There are also substantial communities outside London, for example in Manchester, Leeds and Glasgow. Although the population has declined since its peak in the early twentieth century, there are now about 300,000 Jewish people in Britain, approximately two-thirds of whom live in Greater London. They belong to a range of different strands of Judaism and support many important charitable and community organisations.

The establishment of the State of Israel in 1948 encouraged several thousand British Jews to emigrate there. Meanwhile, Jews from areas such as Aden, India, Iran and Iraq have settled in Britain. Often leaving their homelands because of antagonism sparked by anti-Israel hostility, each group has brought its own distinctive customs and traditions to enrich British Jewish life and culture.

Jewish society in Britain today is lively, with a vibrant array of cultural and educational activities. Jewish people are well represented in all walks of life, from politics and the arts to business and the professions. As one of the oldest minority groups in Britain, the Jewish community is proud to take its place in today's culturally diverse, multi-ethnic, multi-faith society.

*Above:*
**L&D FOODS, HAMPSTEAD GARDEN SUBURB**
Ian Lillicrapp, London, *c.*1990
Photograph
Cutting smoked salmon in a Jewish delicatessen.

*Below:*
**BEVIS MARKS SYNAGOGUE**
Ian Lillicrapp, London, 2004
Photograph
View of the interior of Bevis Marks, looking toward the ark.

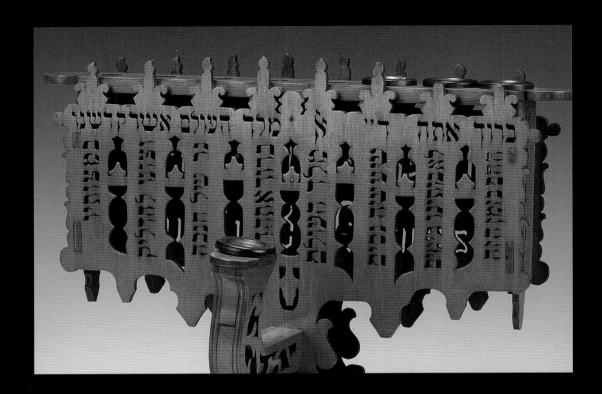

# JEWISH
# RELIGIOUS LIFE

Judaism represents a way of life, practised in the home
as well as the synagogue. The customs and rituals that
mark the yearly cycle of festivals and the rites of
passage from cradle to grave take place in these two
complementary locations. The principle of *hiddur
mitzvah*, enhancing or beautifying the commandment,
encourages the use of artefacts as beautiful as can be
obtained or afforded.

# THE SYNAGOGUE

The synagogue occupies a central position in Jewish community life. It originated as a meeting-house (*bet-knesset*), which incorporated places for study (*bet-midrash*) and prayer (*bet-tefilah*). From it have sprung two great descendants – the church and the mosque.

The basic furniture of the synagogue includes an ark, a large cupboard which in Western communities is placed at the eastern wall, so that the congregation faces towards Jerusalem; in private rooms used for worship it is customary to place a design or picture, known as a *mizrach*, on the east wall in order to show the direction in which to face when praying.

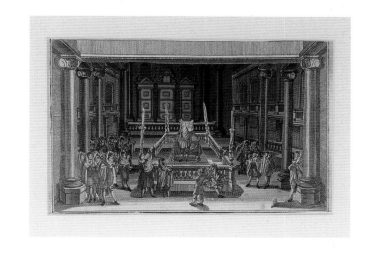

*Above:*
**PEEPSHOW OF A SYNAGOGUE**
Martin Engelbrecht, Augsburg, *c.*1755
Paper
270 mm deep x 150 mm wide
Peepshow formed from six pieces on slotted base. It shows a synagogue interior with *bimah* (reading desk), ark and reader raising the Torah scroll.
C 2000.5

*Left:*
**PANEL BEARING THE TEN COMMANDMENTS**
England, early nineteenth century
Wood
1.04 x 0.73 m
Painted panel from Falmouth Synagogue.
JM 13

In the ark are kept the scrolls of the Law (Torah), covered with a mantle and adorned with ornaments, usually of silver. There is also a reading desk on a raised platform (known as *bimah* in Ashkenazi communities, or *tebah* among Sephardim), a perpetual lamp (*ner tamid*) in front of the ark, and seats for worshippers. Among Orthodox Jews women and men are seated separately.

In front of the ark hangs a curtain of rich material, often beautifully embroidered. In Ashkenazi communities the curtain is hung in front of the doors, but the Sephardi custom is to have the curtains inside. These curtains, like the mantles used to cover the Torah scrolls, are in some cases made from dresses or domestic textiles donated to the synagogue by the ladies of the community.

*Above:*
**MIZRACH**
Place of origin and date unknown
Mahogany, paper, glass
830 x 760 mm
Rectangular *mizrach* surmounted with scrolls centring on a vase of flowers. Two floral arches at top left and right contain pictures of Moses and Aaron, flanking a central arch with a Hebrew inscription:
'I have set the Lord before me always; East' (Psalm 16:8). Larger arches below contain the Ten Commandments in Hebrew.
JM 8

*Right:*
**HANGING LAMP**
Eastern, 1694, with alterations
*c.*1850
Glass, metal, plaster
918 x 297 mm
Round lamp with a flaring tip, suspended by glass chains from a cap designed to catch smoke. The cap is inscribed with Arabic-style letters, and the lamp itself with Hebrew texts from the conclusion of the Sabbath service. The handles, metal base and candle-holder were added later, to convert the lamp from burning oil to candles.
JM 369

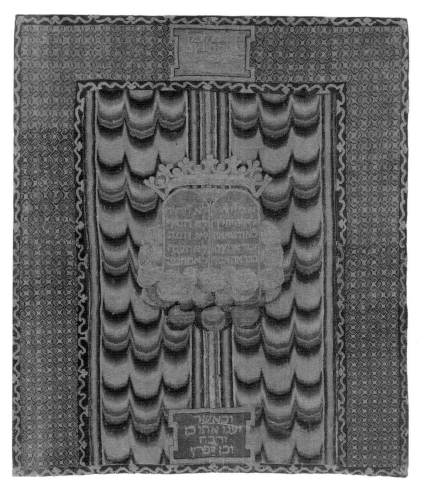

*Above left:*

**ARK CURTAIN**

England (?), late seventeenth to
early eighteenth century
Canvas, wool
1.67 x 1.96 x 0.78 m
Framed and glazed canvas
curtain embroidered in wool, in
brick stitch and gros point. In
the centre are embroidered the
Tablets of the Law with the
Commandments in Hebrew.
The wide border of interlacing
decoration in green, red and
pink is very similar to the
decoration of table carpets of
the late seventeenth or early
eighteenth century.
JM 33

*Above right:*

**ARK CURTAIN**

France, with embroidery
probably from southern
Germany, *c.*1740
Silk damask, silk thread, silver
thread, sequins
2.06 x 1.33 m
White damask embroidered in
coloured silks and silver thread.
The main features of the design
are worked in silver thread,
sequins and panels of brick
stitch. The floral motifs are
worked in polychrome silks.
There is a border of interlacing
ribbons and a long silver-gilt
fringe. Panel of later silk along
the upper edge.
JM 36

*Opposite:*
**ARK**
Italy (Venice?), seventeenth century
Walnut, oak
3.05 x 2.01 x 1.07 m
Carved and gilded synagogue ark, made from walnut wood; the back is a later addition, made from oak. The supporting pillars are painted to imitate marble. Four panels carry carved Jewish emblems: on the left side, the Rod of Aaron; on the left door, the seven-branched *Menorah* and the Ark of the Covenant; on the right door, the bronze basin for priestly ablutions and the table for the Showbread; and on the right side, the Pot of Manna.
JM 14

*Above:*
**ARK CURTAIN AND PELMET**
Germany, *c.*1875
Silk velvet, silver thread, silver wire
Curtain 1.86 x 1.44 m;
pelmet 0.325 x 1.55 m
Saffron-coloured silk velvet curtain embroidered with silver thread, wire and silver plaques with some raised motifs. At the top a pair of two-tailed lions uphold a crown. The formal pattern of ears of corn around the edges of the curtain and along the pelmet suggests that the velvet was originally part of a window- or bed-curtain.
JM 50a

The large synagogue ark that forms the focal point of the museum's ceremonial art displays (JM 14) was discovered by an antiquarian bookseller attending an auction sale at Chillingham Castle in Northumbria, where it had been used as a wardrobe in a steward's bedroom. It was purchased as one of the Museum's earliest exhibits and, when restored, found to date from the seventeenth century and to be of Italian origin, probably from a Venetian synagogue.

The scrolls of the Law, kept inside the ark, are hand-written on parchment by a special scribe and wound round a pair of wooden rollers. When not in use, they are bound together and covered with a mantle, with the tops of the rollers often ornamented by decorative finials, usually in the form of silver ornaments hung with bells (*rimmonim*, literally 'pomegranates'). The bells are sometimes replaced by a crown, particularly in Central Europe. Among Eastern communities it is usual to keep the scroll in a hinged container of silver or wood, known as a *tik*, instead of using a mantle. In some communities it is customary to hang an inscribed silver shield (breast-plate) on the scroll. This may have movable inset plates to indicate the occasion on which the opened portion of the scroll is to be read.

*Above:*
**TORAH MANTLE**
Silk probably made in Spitalfields, 1738–40
Mantle *c.*1750–75
Silk, twill
813 mm high (excluding fringe)
Mantle made from good-quality dress material of the period. The design is of large, naturalistic flowers and leaves in tan, blue, strawberry pink, green and yellow on a white ground. Much of the design was formerly shaded with black silk, now almost completely worn away. (Picture also shows a pair of English *rimmonim*, JM 128.)
JM 64

*Right:*
**SALOMONS TORAH MANTLE**
Italy, 1833
Velvet, silk, silver-gilt thread, sequins
838 mm high (excluding fringe)
Green Torah mantle embroidered with the Salomons coat of arms (possibly by Victor Abraham). The Hebrew inscription, 'Joshua Feibel, son of the late Joseph', is thought to refer to Joseph Salomons, a merchant of Cullum Street. From the Hambro Synagogue.
JM 81

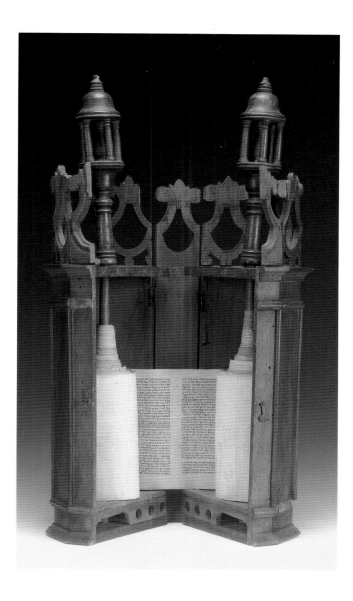

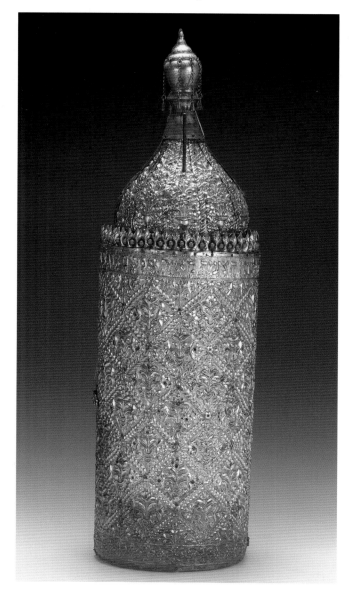

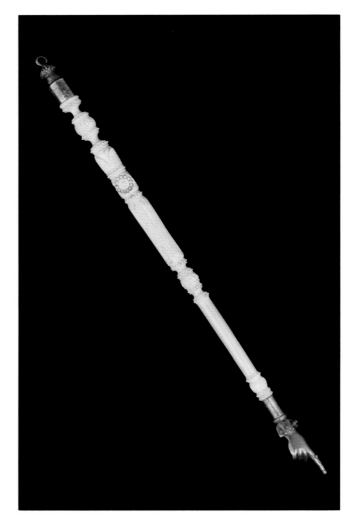

When in use, the scrolls are placed on the reading desk and the reader uses a pointer, usually of silver or occasionally ivory, in the shape of a pointing hand (*yad*), to mark the place and to avoid touching the scroll with his finger.

The word 'Torah' means 'teaching'. At its simplest it refers to the Five Books of Moses written on the scrolls in the synagogue ark, but it is also a comprehensive term that covers all Jewish teaching and tradition, including the Talmud. The Torah, in the wider sense, comprises both the oral and written law and is regarded as a blueprint for observant Jewish life and the source of all Jewish practice and belief.

The oral law was codified as the Talmud, comprising the *Mishnah* (second century) and the *Gemara* (sixth century). Later texts added commentaries and explanations to create *Halachah*, Jewish law, (literally 'The Way'), which develops constantly as new questions arise.

*Above left:*
**TORAH BREAST-PLATE**
France or Italy, early nineteenth century
Silver
292 x 195 mm
Shield-shaped breast-plate chased with Tablets of the Law surrounded by a pierced laurel wreath, joined by floral links to a large coronet, with two suspension chains.
JM 146

*Above:*
**TORAH POINTER**
Place of origin unknown, nineteenth century
Silver-gilt, ivory, precious stones
282 mm long
Turned ivory shaft carved with foliage. Silver-gilt hand and cuff set with stones, and silver-gilt finial.
JM 178

# DAILY LIFE

Observant Jews recite prayers three times a day. The main components are the *Shema*, which expresses the fundamentals of Jewish belief, and the A*midah* or 'standing prayer'. The *Shema* is said twice a day, in the morning and evening, and consists of three paragraphs taken from the Five Books of Moses. Its opening line, 'Hear O Israel, the Lord our God, the Lord is One' (Deuteronomy 6:4), emphasises the nature of Judaism as a monotheistic religion. The *mitzvot* (commandments), contained in the *Shema*, are part of daily life and include *tefillin*, *mezuzah* and *tzitzit*.

The observant Jewish male wears *tefillin* (phylacteries) for daily morning prayers, except on Sabbath and festivals. Two square boxes, containing small parchment scrolls with four passages from the Torah, are bound by leather straps to the forehead and left arm respectively.

*Above:*
**SPANISH DAILY PRAYER BOOK**
Printed by David Tartas,
Amsterdam, 1690s
Paper, tortoiseshell, silver
153 x 114 mm
Daily Prayer Book, Torah and *Haftarot* printed in Spanish 'for ladies and persons unfamiliar with Hebrew'.
C 1973.1.22.1

*Left:*
***TEFILLIN* CASES**
Germany, late eighteenth or early nineteenth century
Silver
Each 9.5 mm wide
Cubic cases with Hebrew inscriptions over four sides, highly decorated with engraved motifs, on spreading bases with hinged covers.
Maker's mark: 'JM'.
JM 583 & 583a

The *mezuzah* is a narrow container holding the *Shema*, written on parchment, and is fixed to the right door-posts of the entrance and rooms in a Jewish home. Some people have the custom of kissing the *mezuzah* when they enter and leave, remembering the instruction within it to 'Love the Lord your God with all your heart, all your soul and all your strength'.

The third paragraph of the *Shema* contains instructions about *tzitzit* (fringes), which are found in two versions. The larger is the *tallit* or prayer-shawl, which is worn during prayers. It is traditionally made of cream cloth with black stripes, but silk shawls with blue stripes are worn in some communities. Different colours and weaves are becoming popular today. The smaller version is the *arba kanfot* ('four corners'), which is generally worn by observant men under their clothing. The fringes are taken out and kissed when the *Shema* is said, as looking at them is a means of remembering the *mitzvot*.

*Right:*
**SUNDIAL**
Pisa, 1765
Bronze
121 mm high
Miniature standing sundial on circular foot. Shaped dial plate with pierced gnomon. Inscribed in Hebrew: 'The Noonday Prayer at his hour forget thou not to say.'
JM 576

*Below:*
**ARBA KANFOT**
Leeds, *c.*1900
Cotton
*c.*600 mm long
Child's *arba kanfot* crocheted in yellow and cream yarn; such bright colours would be very unusual if the *arba kanfot* were intended for an adult.
C 1995.3

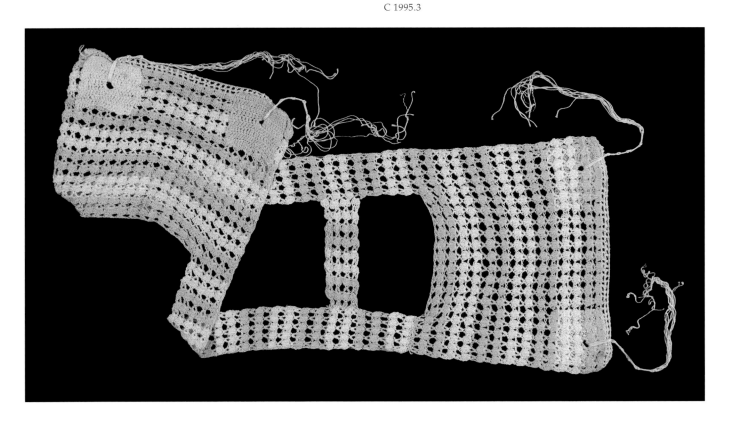

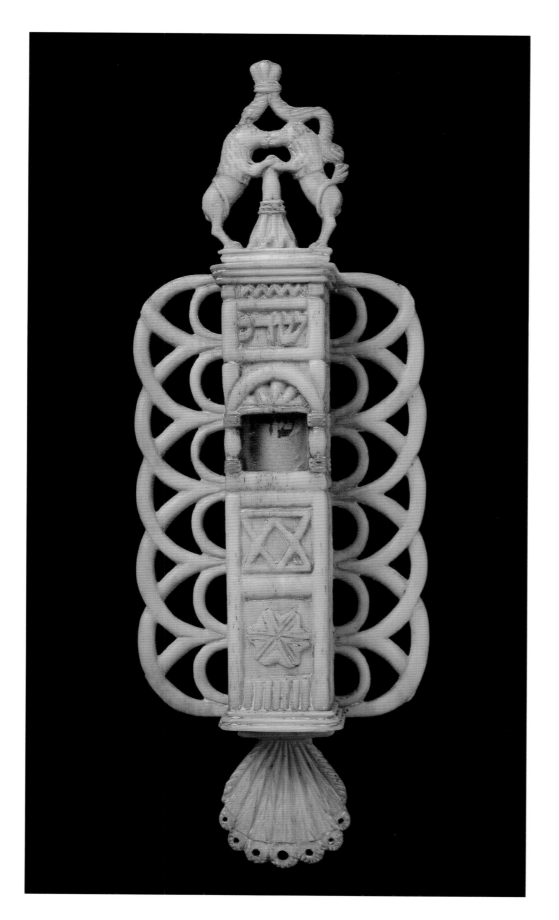

**MEZUZAH**

Italy, fifteenth to sixteenth century

Bone

189 mm high

Polished bone *mezuzah* centred on an oblong case of square section, carved with Hebrew characters and geometric motifs. Above are two lions rampant affronté under a canopy, below is a shell pendant, and at the sides are interlaced arches. Traces of paint remain on the cover.

JM 585

*Kashrut*, the dietary laws derived from the Torah relating to the preparation and consumption of permitted foods, is central to Jewish life. Observant Jews only eat animals that have split hooves and chew the cud, and fish that have fins and scales. Mammals and poultry must be killed using a special method called *shechita*, which ensures that death is instantaneous. Before cooking, meats and poultry have to be soaked and salted to remove as much blood as possible. In addition, meat and milk foods are cooked separately and never served at the same meal. As well as these general laws, there are certain foods traditionally associated with particular festivals. As modern convenience foods contain vast numbers of additives, which may not be *kosher*, Jews who are particular about *kashrut* will read food labels carefully, and may only feel happy eating food that has been prepared at home or under rabbinical supervision.

# THE SABBATH

The celebration of the Sabbath (*Shabbat*), the weekly day of rest, is one of the most important aspects of Jewish life in the home. The Sabbath is welcomed in at sunset on Friday by the woman of the household lighting the Sabbath candles or an oil lamp. A blessing is then recited over wine, which is drunk from a special *kiddush* cup. After the ceremonial washing of hands, a special plaited bread called *hallah* is blessed and eaten by the family, followed by a festive meal.

The main synagogue service takes place on Saturday morning, when each week, as on other holy days, a certain portion of the Torah is read. The day is enjoyed in quiet relaxation. After dark, when there are three stars in the sky, the end of the Sabbath is marked by the *Havdalah* (distinction) ceremony. Blessings are said over wine, a plaited candle and fragrant spices, to thank God for the senses of taste, sight and smell and to symbolise the difference between the day of rest and the six working days. Special spice containers were created for use in the *Havdalah* ceremony. A popular form of spice container is the silver spice tower, whose shape is an echo of the towers in which spices were stored in medieval times.

*Above:*
**PLATE**
Lambeth Factory, London,
mid-eighteenth century
Ceramic, tin-glaze
250 mm diameter
Delftware plate with the Hebrew
word *basar* in the centre,
indicating that it is to be used
for meat-based rather than
milk-based meals. Stylised floral
and leaf designs on border.
C 1982.10.19.1

*Above:*
**SPICE BOX**
Germany, seventeenth to
eighteenth century
Pewter
45 x 70 x 67 mm
Square box on four hoof feet.
Three sides pierced with geometric
ornament. Sliding cover with scroll
handle, punched with Hebrew
characters. Interior has four
divisions. Maker's mark: an angel.
JM 411

*Right:*
**KIDDUSH CUP**
Gerald Benney, Beenham House workshops, Berkshire, 1997
Gold, silver, enamel
109 mm high
Gold and silver cup decorated with an enamelled Tree of Life motif in green and brown. Maker's mark: 'AGB' (Adrian Gerald Benney).
C 2000.6

*Below:*
**CANDLESTICK WITH SPICE DRAWER**
Germany, eighteenth century
Silver
310 mm high
*Havdalah* candlestick and spice container set on a circular, domed, partly fluted base with crimmed rim; the unusual stem takes the form of a man holding a wine cup and a tray, supporting with his head the square openwork spice section, which is fitted with a drawer; this is surmounted by a movable platform serving as a candle holder, set within a frame of four wire supports, which terminate in small spherical knobs.
C 1988.49

*Left:*
**KIDDUSH CUP**
Germany, 1678
Silver
74 mm high
Small goblet with octagonal upper part, engraved with flowers, fruit, the initials 'HB' (possibly a maker's mark) and the date. Cylindrical lower part embossed with apple-like fruit, on a scalloped base.
JM 383

**SABBATH LAMP**
Abraham de Oliveyra, London,
1734
Silver
797 mm high
Sephardi-style lamp in six parts:
hook, crown, large ball, reservoir
with seven burners, circular drip
bowl and acorn pendant.
JM 373

The earliest known type of special Sabbath lamp dates
back to the fourteenth century. It is a hanging lamp to which a
star-shaped oil container is attached, and below which a
receptacle for dripping oil is suspended. This was known in
Germany as the *Judenstern* or 'Jew's Star'. It was made mainly
in brass, but examples exist in pewter and, more rarely, silver.
Another type of Sabbath lamp, also made in silver, brass and
pewter, was common in Sephardi communities in England and
the Netherlands, and seems to have been in use during the
seventeenth and eighteenth centuries. It has at least five parts,
each one suspended below the next, the top usually being in
the form of a crown. One example in silver (JM 373), made in
London in 1734, is by Abraham de Oliveyra, an Anglo-Jewish
silversmith whose work is well represented in the Museum.

However, candlesticks have been the most common form
of Sabbath light (especially in northern Europe) since the
nineteenth century, and probably even earlier. These were
usually no different from ordinary candlesticks, and it is rare to
find examples with specifically Jewish characteristics.

# THE YEARLY CYCLE: FESTIVALS AND HOLY DAYS

The Jewish year follows a lunar calendar, with the interpolation of an additional month according to a specified cycle to bring it into alignment with the solar calendar. This means that the Jewish festivals and holy days, which always fall on the same dates in the Hebrew calendar, move slightly from year to year in relation to the Gregorian calendar.

## Rosh Hashanah and Yom Kippur

The New Year (*Rosh Hashanah*), which falls on 1 *Tishri*, during the autumn, and the Day of Atonement (*Yom Kippur*), which follows it ten days later, are the most solemn days of the Jewish year. On *Rosh Hashanah* the *shofar*, a trumpet made from a ram's horn, is blown, a custom originating in biblical times that has continued ever since. The *shofar* is an ancient Jewish symbol and occurs on Jewish coins and in wall paintings and sculpture found in ancient synagogues. Its sound acts as a reminder to people that a new year is beginning and that they have an opportunity to atone for their sins and to make a fresh start in the year ahead. During the 'ten days of penitence' between *Rosh Hashanah* and *Yom Kippur* special prayers are said, asking forgiveness for any wrongdoing. The Day of Atonement is a day of fasting, and prayers continue all day. Finally the *shofar* is blown as a signal that the fast is over and that forgiveness is granted. At this time of year the ark curtain and Torah covers are white, to symbolise purity, and it is also traditional to wear white on *Yom Kippur*.

*Below:*
**YOM KIPPUR ARK CURTAIN**
Place of origin and date unknown
Velvet, gold thread
1.15 x 0.79 m
White velvet ark curtain embroidered with gold thread. At the top is a crown; at the centre is a sun symbol containing a *shofar*. These are surrounded by inscriptions relating to the motifs and a frame of foliage.
JM 208

*Right:*
**SHOFAR**
Place of origin unknown, eighteenth century
Horn
482 mm long
*Shofar* engraved with a Hebrew inscription in a frame of foliage: 'Blow the horn on the new moon, at the beginning of the month for our day of festival; for it is a statute for Israel, a decree of the God of Jacob' (Psalm 81: 4–5).
JM 194

# Sukkot

Shortly after the solemn days of *Rosh Hashanah* and *Yom Kippur* comes *Sukkot* (Tabernacles), a harvest festival and a remembrance of the forty years of wandering in the wilderness after the Israelites' exodus from Egypt. It is celebrated for a week, beginning on 15 *Tishri*, and during this time meals are eaten in a temporary booth (*sukkah*), with a roof of leaves and branches decorated with seasonal fruits and flowers. In the synagogue a palm branch with twigs of myrtle and willow bound together (*lulav*) is carried in one hand and a citron (*etrog*) in the other hand, both representing the autumn harvest. The *etrog* is frequently carried to synagogue in a specially designed box. Some of the examples on display in the Museum are worked with naturalistic leaves and tendrils.

Sukkot *is* followed by a further two-day festival culminating on 23 *Tishri* in *Simchat Torah*, the Rejoicing of the Law, when the yearly cycle of the reading of the Torah is completed and begins again. The Torah scrolls are carried round the synagogue seven times in procession, and the day is celebrated with song, dance and festivity.

*Above:*
**SUKKAH PEEPSHOW**
Place of origin unknown, eighteenth century
Paper, wood
236 mm high, 297 mm deep
Scene in a *sukkah*, with five movable frames.
JM 210

*Left:*
**PROCESSION OF THE LAW**
Solomon Alexander Hart RA
England, *c.*1845–50
Oil on canvas
1.06 x 0.94 m
Painting showing a synagogue scene at the festival of *Simchat Torah*, believed to be set in the synagogue at Livorno, Italy.
C 1974.2.25.3

*Left:*
**ETROG BOX**
Germany or Austria (?),
date unknown
Silver
277 mm long
Box formed as a citron with
applied foliage and tendril;
stand formed as a leaf.
JM 215

*Below:*
**ETROG BOX**
Mila Tanya Griebel, London,
2001
Silver
200 x 100 mm
Box in a double-cone shape
with cut-out letters.
C 2001.3

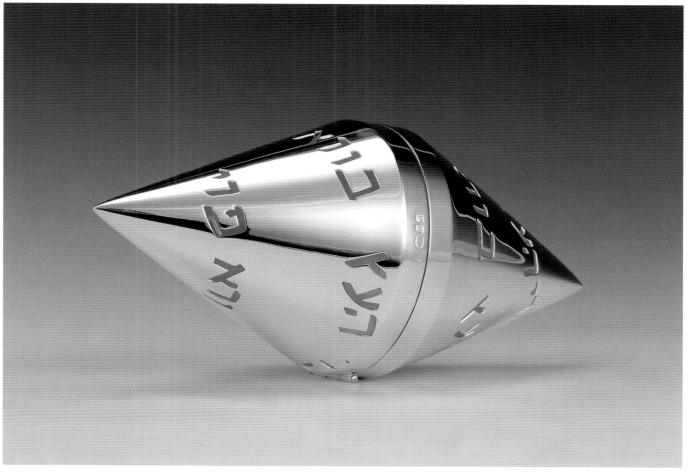

**HANUKAH LAMP**

Moses Haso, Germany (Altona?), *c.*1770
Silver, parcel gilt
594 x 324 mm

Backplate formed as an Ark of the Law, with central hinged doors flanked by columns, and a coronet above. Doors open to disclose a Hebrew inscription giving the blessing for lighting *Hanukah* lights. Cresting above bears an applied cartouche and vase of flowers flanked by griffins, with a large shell at the top. The main columns are surmounted by lions, and the burners decorated with dolphin masks. The shaped apron below is chased with a figure lighting the *Hanukah* lamp at the top of a flight of steps, before two other figures.

JM 242

# Hanukah

*Hanukah* (the Festival of Lights) is celebrated for eight days in December, beginning on 25 *Kislev*. It commemorates the victory of the Maccabeans, a small group of Jews led by Judah Maccabeus, over the army of Antiochus Epiphanes, the Greek king of Syria, in 165 BCE. Antiochus had tried to destroy the Jewish religion, and the Maccabeans' first task was to re-dedicate the Temple, which had been desecrated by the Greeks. According to tradition, although there was only enough oil in the Temple to light the *Menorah* (Temple lamp) for one day, it lasted for eight days, until more oil could be obtained. In celebration of this miracle a lamp with eight lights is lit with the aid of the moveable ninth light (the *shammas*), beginning with one light on the first night and adding another each night until all eight are lit.

The *Hanukah* lamp is probably the most widely known of all Jewish ritual objects. It is used both in the home and in the synagogue, where the standing nine-branched lamp, the type with which most people are familiar, is commonly found. The lamp stands to the right of the ark, where the seven-branched light stood in the Temple of Jerusalem, and its shape recalls that of the Temple *Menorah* as shown on ancient monuments. There are many different styles of *Hanukah* lamp for the home, often reflecting the period and country in which they were made. For example, lamps made in Italy during the sixteenth and seventeenth centuries reflect the tastes of the Renaissance and Baroque periods and are often decorated with cherubs and sirens. Later sumptuous examples boast menageries of heraldic beasts.

*Right:*

**HANUKAH LAMP**

Netherlands, mid-eighteenth century
Pewter
287 x 263 mm

Shaped backplate with shell cresting, flanked by demi-figures, and engraved below with a wrigglework tulip. Drip buckets are suspended from inverted dolphin spouts, above a shaped pan with large paw feet. Maker's mark: a female figure dancing with initials ('ADA'?) above.

JM 262

*Opposite:*

**HANUKAH LAMP**

Moshe Leser, Tarnów, *c.*1936
Plywood, copper
290 x 270 x 185 mm

Fretwork lamp with silhouetted griffins flanking openwork design on base; other parts are decorated with Hebrew and German Gothic lettering. The lamp and matching *mezuzah* were made as a wedding gift for Leser's son, who had settled in England.

C 1988.18

# Purim

The festival of *Purim* is held on 14 *Adar*, in the early spring, and commemorates the deliverance of the Persian Jews during the reign of King Ahasuerus (thought to be Xerxes, who reigned from 485 to 465 BCE). The dramatic story of Esther and Mordecai is told in the Book of Esther, which is read on this day from a special scroll known as a *Megillah*. Since the name of God is not mentioned in the Book of Esther, it was considered permissible for anyone, even a child, to write and illustrate it, although the scrolls for synagogal use were not illustrated. In Italy especially, scrolls for domestic use were lavishly decorated with scenes from the story, and there are a number of professionally engraved scrolls from seventeenth- and eighteenth-century Italy and the Netherlands. To hold the scrolls special cases were made, in silver, gold or ivory, which were often decorated with scenes from the Book of Esther. Another frequent decoration is that of a fish, the symbol of the month of *Adar* (Pisces) in which the holiday occurs. Some of these are beautiful examples of the art of the silversmith and capture the joyous spirit of the festival, which is celebrated with elements of carnival, such as fancy dress, play-acting, music and dancing. In all communities charity is given to the poor and special collection boxes or plates are placed in the synagogue.

**MEGILLAH PARCHMENT ON RED SILK** (detail)
Italy, seventeenth century
Vellum
*c*.2.3 m long
Cut-out vellum *Megillah* scroll with designs of griffins, human figures, animals and landscape scenes, mounted on a red silk backing.
JM 284

*Right:*

**MEGILLAH**

Netherlands, nineteenth century
Silver, parchment
Case 209 mm long;
scroll 999 x 81 mm

Case formed as a fish,
symbolising the Zodiac sign of
Pisces, for the month of *Adar*.
The scroll emerges from between
the fins, with a shaft for winding
issuing from the tail.
JM 317

*Below right:*

**MEGILLAH**

Galicia, Poland, *c.*1750
Silver, silver-gilt, parchment
Case 203 mm long; scroll
1.62 x 0.17 m

Cylindrical case, pierced and
chased with flowers on gilt
lining. Finished with a baluster
finial and pear-shaped handle.
Silver edging mount to scroll,
with figure of a running squirrel.
JM 298

# Pesach

*Pesach* (Passover) is one of the principal festivals of the Jewish year. It recalls the liberation of the Israelites from their slavery under the Pharaohs in Egypt in the late second millennium BCE. The festival begins on 15 *Nisan*, which usually occurs during April, and lasts for eight days. During this period the only bread that may be eaten is unleavened (*matzah*), as a reminder of the flat bread baked in haste by the Israelites before their hurried departure from Egypt. The home is carefully cleaned to ensure that no traces of food containing yeast (*chametz*) remain, culminating in a search carried out with a candle to check for any stray crumbs hidden away in a dark corner.

The highlight of the festival is the opening meal or *Seder*, which takes place in the home on the first two nights of *Pesach*, although in Israel and in Reform Jewish homes only one *Seder* is held. At the *Seder* the story of the exodus from Egypt is read from a special prayer book called a *Haggadah*. Since medieval times the *Haggadah* has been lavishly illustrated, in both manuscript and printed versions. Special *Seder* plates are used to contain symbolic foods, such as bitter herbs and salt water, which recall the years of slavery in Egypt.

*Above:*

**ILLUSTRATION FROM *HAGGADAH* AND SONG OF SONGS**
Hamy Bekhor, Cairo, 1929
Vellum, velvet
320 x 270 mm
Handwritten *Haggadah* and Song of Songs in Sephardi Hebrew script. Hand-sewn and bound in velvet, with a blue velvet case. The artist included this illustration of a piano as a reference to his family's connection with the piano trade.
C 1989.3

*Right:*

**SEDER PLATE**
Italy (Savona?), early seventeenth century, or The Hague (Rosenberg Factory), late nineteenth century
Faience
486 mm diameter
Hebrew inscription relating to the Passover service in centre. Sunken panels on flange with figures of Moses, Aaron, David and Solomon, a *Seder* table and a scene of the selling of Joseph.
JM 339

*Opposite:*

**CUP OF ELIJAH**
Bohemia, nineteenth century
Glass, gold leaf
250 x 80 mm
A wine cup for the prophet Elijah is traditionally placed on the Passover *Seder* table. This lidded cup was produced using the *Zwischengoldglas* technique (also called *verre eglomisé*), in which gold leaf is placed between two layers of glass. It is decorated with illustrations from the life of Elijah, dressed in Galician style, in reverse foil engraving on gold leaf.
C 1999.2.77

Pewter *Seder* plates, often with inscriptions and symbolic decorations, were very popular in Germany from the seventeenth century to the nineteenth, although silver versions are also known. Ceramic plates are also known to have been used in Italy and England. It is customary to recline while eating, and occasionally there are special cushions for this purpose.

*Above:*
**SEDER PLATE**
Designed by Mark Tepper for Ridgeways,
Staffordshire, c.1850–1910
Ceramic
263 mm diameter
Inscribed in Hebrew and English with
the order of the Passover *Seder*
ceremony, and, in the centre, the special
symbolic foods.
JM 356

## Shavuot

The festival of *Shavuot* (the Feast of Weeks or Pentecost) celebrates the divine revelation of the giving of the Torah, and takes place on 6 *Sivan*. The Bible records how, seven weeks after the exodus from Egypt, the Ten Commandments were given to Moses and the Children of Israel at Mount Sinai. *Shavuot* is also associated with the wheat harvest and the offering of the first fruits at the Temple in ancient times. The Book of Ruth, with its reference to the harvest, is read at this festival. The seven-week period between the festivals of *Pesach* and *Shavuot* is called the *Omer*. This time span is counted day by day in the synagogue on a board, which is often gaily decorated.

*Above:*
**OMER CALENDAR**
Place of origin unknown, eighteenth
century
Mahogany, paper, glass
378 x 284 mm
Glass-fronted frame containing a scroll,
turning on two rollers, marked with three
rows of numbers representing the days,
weeks and months of the *Omer*.
JM 363a

**BOOK OF RUTH, PLATE 1**

Maty Grünberg (using a translation by
Linda Zisquit), England, 1996
Paper
583 x 476 x 48 mm
Plate from one of a limited edition of
125 portfolios containing the Book
of Ruth, illustrated with black and colour
woodcuts, hand-printed by the artist
on an 1860 Albion press.
C 1997.5

# THE LIFE CYCLE

Each event in the Jewish life cycle is marked by religious ritual, often enriched by tradition.

## Birth

When a new baby is named, the blessing is made that he or she should grow up to the *Torah* (religious study), *huppah* (marriage) and a life of *ma'asim tovim* (good deeds). The latter includes ethical *mitzvot* (commandments) such as performing acts of charity, and ritual *mitzvot* such as observing *tefillin* *tzitzit* and *mezuzah*. Amulets were often used to protect the small baby and newly delivered mother from harm. The rite of circumcision (the Covenant of Abraham) is fundamental to Judaism and goes back to the religion's origins. It is performed by a specially trained person (*mohel*) on baby boys when they are eight days old. The baby is placed on a cushion held in the arms of a godfather (*sandak*), who sits in a special chair. In some European towns the ceremony took place in the synagogue, where there was often a chair with two seats known as the 'Chair of Elijah' which was used during the ceremony. A custom among the Jews of Germany and some surrounding areas was for the baby to be swaddled in a special binder (*wimpel*), embroidered or painted with the child's name and date of birth, often whimsically decorated. When the child paid his first visit to the synagogue, he presented it as a binder for the Torah scrolls. At the time of *Barmitzvah* for a boy (age thirteen), or *Batmitzvah* for a girl (age twelve), a Jewish child takes on full responsibility for keeping *mitzvot*.

**TWO MARRIAGE RINGS**
*(Left)* Italy, seventeenth century
Silver-gilt
27 mm diameter
Hoop chased with Hebrew inscription and formal flowers on a matted ground, with corded borders.
JM 461

*(Right)* Italy, early seventeenth century
Gold
46 mm high (including bezel)
Hoop pierced with two rows of circles outlined in filigree wire and corded borders. Bezel formed as a hexagonal building with pilasters at angles and domed roof with Hebrew inscription, one letter on each side.
JM 456

# Marriage

The Jewish wedding ceremony traditionally takes place under a *huppah* (canopy) and may be performed anywhere. Although it was formerly more common for it to be held in the open air or in a private home, nowadays it often takes place in a synagogue. The groom puts a ring on the bride's finger, and a traditional formula and blessings are recited. Most of the rings on display in the Museum were probably used during this ceremony and may not have been the property of individuals. These were often very elaborate pieces of jewellery with filigree decoration and enamelling and were ornamented with little houses as bezels. Almost invariably found on them are the Hebrew words for 'good luck' (*Mazal Tov*). Gifts between bride and groom, known as *sivlonot*, included prayer books in silver bindings or a silver marriage belt.

The *ketubah* or marriage contract, setting out the bridegroom's obligations to his bride, is signed by the parties concerned and at least two witnesses. The contract is written in accordance with a custom that dates back to the first century BCE, in the Aramaic language, used by Jews in addition to Hebrew. The document is kept by the bride or her family and may be lavishly illuminated.

*Above:*
**MARRIAGE BELT**
Place of origin unknown, mid-sixteenth century
Gold and other metal
900 mm long
Gilded belt with sets of chains linking bosses alternating with rosettes.
Decorated with images of marriage rings with bezels shaped as buildings.
C 2003.4

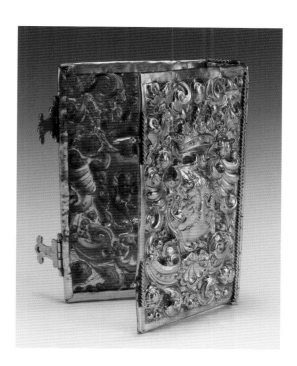

*Left:*
**PRAYER BOOK COVER**
Venice, *c.*1715
Silver
165 x 150 x 32 mm
Book cover, repoussé and chased
with a coat of arms surmounted
by coronets and surrounded by
scrolling foliage, with a Hebrew
inscription. Maker's mark:
'HONOR'.
C 1999.2.67

*Right:*
***KETUBAH***
Calcutta, 1895
Paper
250 x 330 mm
Illuminated Baghdadi-Indian
*ketubah* recording the marriage
of David, the son of Shaul
David, to Simha, the daughter
of Joseph Sassoon.
C 2003.2

# Death

There is a great reverence for the human body in death. The deceased must be buried in a proper state, and it is a pious duty to wash and prepare the body for this purpose. To undertake this task, a group of members of the community joined together in a society known as the *Hevra Kadisha* (holy fellowship). It was considered an honour to belong to such a group and a blessing to carry out the tasks for the dead. These groups also met on other occasions, and there are a number of special wine beakers and cups in the Museum that were used by the members of a *Hevra Kadisha*; often the names of the members were engraved on them. A lamp is lit in the home each year on the anniversary (*yahrzeit*) of the death of a close relative.

*Above:*
**PRINTED SUMMONS
TO A BURIAL SOCIETY**
Netherlands, 1893
Card
120 x 120 mm
Printed card in Portuguese and Hebrew, partly completed in ink, summoning Isaac de Silva of Amsterdam of the Holy Brotherhood of Loving Kindness and Faith to prepare the body of Isaac Bueno de Mesquita for burial.
JM 573

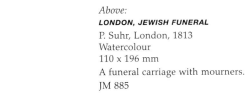

*Above:*
**LONDON, JEWISH FUNERAL**
P. Suhr, London, 1813
Watercolour
110 x 196 mm
A funeral carriage with mourners.
JM 885

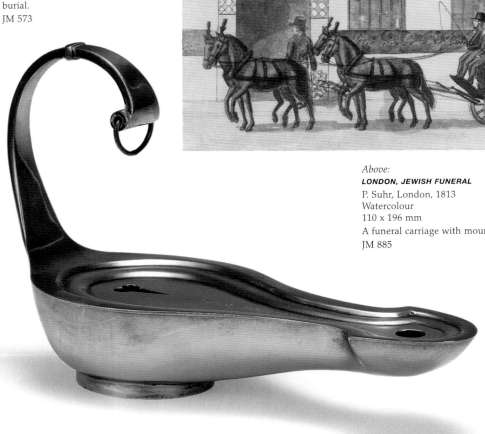

*Left:*
**YAHRZEIT LAMP**
Messrs S. J. Phillips, London, 1903
Silver
196 mm long
Memorial lamp of classical form inscribed in Hebrew with the fifth commandment: 'Honour thy father and thy mother' (Exodus 10:12).
JM 575

# Tzedakah

*Tzedakah*, the Hebrew word for charity, means literally 'justice'. Helping those in need is not seen solely as an act of personal generosity but also as part of an obligation to bring fairness to the world, in partnership with God. *Tzedakah* may take many forms. One of the most important is the *tzedakah* of kindness and respect for others. It is a *mitzvah* to give practical help, visit the sick, accompany the dead to the cemetery and comfort mourners.

The most common form of *tzedakah* is donations to provide financial support for the less fortunate and for the institutions that care for them. The collecting box is a familiar sight in Jewish homes and businesses.

Through the cycles of daily and weekly rituals, yearly festivals and a commitment to religious values in all aspects of life, observant Jewish people are linked to the rich heritage of their faith.

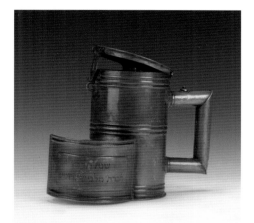

*Left:*
**CHARITY BOX**
Italy (?), 1837
Brass
172 mm high
Cylindrical box with angular handle. Upper half with slot for almsgiving, lower with swivelling compartment for receiving alms. Inscribed in Hebrew with the date and the name of the charity: The Brotherhood for Clothing the Poor.
JM 579

*Right:*
**CHARITY LOTTERY WHEEL**
S. Lazarus, England, 1806
Pine, 1.22 x 0.61 m
Pinewood drum, stained black, mounted on a fluted rectangular open stand. Carved panels on the centre of the drum, four of which have acorn decoration. Hebrew inscription carved in relief round the circumference of the drum and gilded: 'Presented by the founder Meier Hirsch to the Brotherhood for Helping the Poor to [obtain] Their Needs for Sabbath.'
JM 452

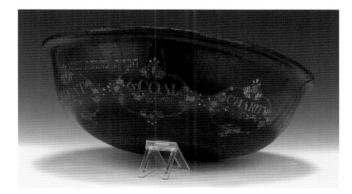

*Above:*
**BREAD, MEAT AND COAL SOCIETY BOWL**
England, nineteenth century
Papier mâché, 116 x 351 mm
Black painted bowl decorated with flowers and inscribed in English and Hebrew. The *Meshebat Nephesh* (Spirit of the Sabbath) Society was the first English Ashkenazi charity, founded in 1779 to provide poor Jews with bread, meat and coal.
C 1999.2.87.2

# A TREASURY OF EUROPEAN GOLDSMITHS' WORK

Anthony Phillips

Unlike so many silver collections in British institutions, that of the Jewish Museum is extraordinarily rich in works made across the length and breadth of Europe over several centuries. The vast majority of items reflect, of course, the various traditions of the Jewish communities and individuals for whom they were made but, though deeply traditional, they inevitably incorporate regional and stylistic influences.

The late Arthur Grimwade, who contributed so much to the study of Anglo-Jewish silver over the years and, in particular, to the silver section of the detailed and informative *Catalogue of the Jewish Museum* published in 1974, put it another way. He wrote in notes for an unpublished lecture: 'the goldsmith, in which term I include the silversmith, has always in making religious objects to achieve a synthesis or balance between the functional and iconographic requirements of the object and the current fashion of the day in ornament and technique.'

The earliest examples of goldsmiths' work in the collection are a small group of Gothic and Renaissance Jewish wedding rings. Inevitably however, given the chances of survival, a far greater proportion of Judaic silver objects are extant from the seventeenth and eighteenth centuries, and these amply demonstrate the changes in ornament and technique that occurred during the Baroque, Rococo and Neoclassical periods, both in European silver as a whole and in Jewish ritual objects in particular.

*Right:*
**TORAH BREAST-PLATE**
Daniel Hammerer, Strasbourg,
*c.*1682
Silver
241 x 191 mm
Oblong plaque fitted to receive sliding interchangeable labels bearing names of festivals in the centre, surrounded by commemorative inscriptions in Hebrew. Engraved *fleur-de-lis* above on each side. Applied corner mounts of cherubs, masks and scrolls, pendant pomegranate and bells below and crown above. Suspension chains joined by double-headed eagle with book.
JM 136

# THE SEVENTEENTH CENTURY

One of the earliest pieces is a rare silver-gilt breast-plate made by Daniel Hammerer, around 1682, in one of the great centres of European goldsmithing, Strasbourg (JM 136). The cast openwork scroll and cherub masks at the angles are typical of this date, and it is tempting to suggest the engraved *fleur-de-lis* may have been added at the time the city became French in 1681. It is interesting to note that Hammerer is also recorded as making a particularly fine Baroque chalice.

The exceptionally rare French laver and ewer (JM 191) made by Jean I Delahaye in Paris, around 1670, typifies the decoration of the Baroque. The border of the oval dish is repoussé and chased with beautifully executed flowers and foliage on a matted ground. The ewer, on a spreading foot with pierced acanthus border, is applied with further acanthus and palm foliage and its cover surmounted by a tulip-formed finial that may perhaps be a replacement. Like many sixteenth- and

*Left:*
**LAVER AND EWER**
Jean I Delahaye, Paris, *c.*1670
Silver
Laver 470 mm wide;
ewer 248 mm high
Oval laver with plain well and decorated border, for washing the hands before the Priestly Blessing. Vase-shaped ewer on circular foot, with harp-shaped handle and long curved spout. Engraved with initials 'MM'.
JM 191

seventeenth-century tankards and cups presented to English churches, this laver and ewer almost certainly started life with a secular function. They would have formed part of a magnificent Louis XIV dressing-table service, along with a mirror, candlesticks, bell and numerous caskets, boxes and bottles. The ewer is similar to that included in a service made in Paris between 1659 and 1669 and now in Rosenborg Castle, Copenhagen, while the basin is almost identical to that in another service at Chatsworth, Derbyshire, made there a year or two later. Presumably the Museum's example was presented to the Hambro Synagogue in the eighteenth century by a wealthy member to be used for the Priestly Blessing.

A further example of late Baroque silversmithing, and one that is absolutely typical of Dutch workmanship of the period, is the beautiful pierced and engraved bookbinding containing the Pentateuch with *Haftarot* printed in 1671 in Amsterdam (JM 187). The piercing is of a somewhat inappropriate nude female figure, which almost certainly represents Venus, with Cupid, cherubs and flowers. These are the sort of secular and classical themes to be found on similarly pierced and engraved Dutch marriage caskets of the period, made to contain coins presented as engagement gifts to the intended by non-Jewish suitors in Friesland and the north of Holland.

**LOUIS XIV DRESSING-TABLE SERVICE**
Paris, 1669–71, most with the maker's
mark of Pierre Provost
Silver
From the Devonshire Collection,
Chatsworth House
Copyright The Devonshire Collection,
Chatsworth. Reproduced by permission of
the Chatsworth Settlement Trustees.

Such regional variations and development of artistic forms in late seventeenth-century silver, supplied both to the synagogue and the home, are particularly well demonstrated by the Museum's exceptional group of *rimmonim* and *Hanukah* lamps. The *rimmonim*, the finials attached to the top of the Torah scrolls, reflect the diversity of their form both in technique and design. Baroque examples demonstrate the considerable contrast between Italian and Dutch silversmithing. A superb Venetian pair, by the unidentified maker AP, is exceptionally richly chased with flowers, foliage, musical trophies and other ornament (JM 103). In sharp contrast is a typical Dutch pair made at roughly the same date, which, though unmarked, was most probably made in Amsterdam (JM 102). These are of classic Dutch architectural form, each on a plain shaft with the lower part of the body hung with bells and pierced and chased with foliage, the upper part formed as a hexagonal tower enclosing further bells. Indeed, Dutch *rimmonim* are of such architectural form as to invite comparisons with the towers of specific buildings in the Netherlands such as the Oude Kirke in Amsterdam and the Weigh-house at Alkmaar.

*Above left:*
**RIMMONIM**
Venice, late seventeenth century
Silver
610 mm high
Hexagonal three-tiered *rimmonim*. Finials formed as vases of flowers. One row of bells at base, with festooned chains between. Maker's mark: 'AP', with a device (orb and cross?) between the letters.
JM 103

*Above right:*
**RIMMONIM**
Netherlands (probably Amsterdam), c.1695
Silver, gilt
476 mm high
Hexagonal three-tiered *rimmonim* of cupola form. Lowest tier bulbous, with matted surface and scroll foliage; central tier architectural; upper tier of foliate scrolls. Pineapple finial. Gilt bells, finials, scroll brackets and cresting.
JM 102

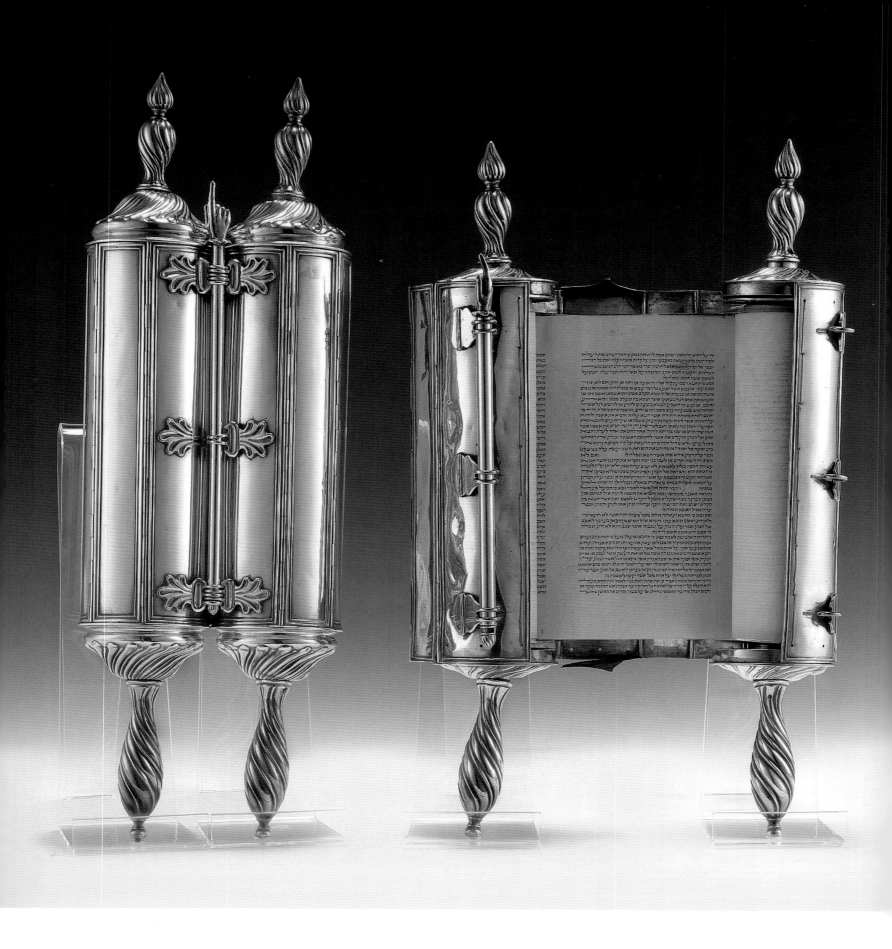

# EIGHTEENTH-CENTURY SYNAGOGUE SILVER

Both the Baroque and the subsequent artistic developments that swept Europe as a whole in the eighteenth century, the asymmetry of the Rococo and the balance and order of the Neoclassical, are well seen in the Museum's English *rimmonim* and a remarkable pair of miniature silver enclosed scrolls. The earliest *rimmonim* are by a Sephardi silversmith, Abraham de Oliveyra, and were made in 1716, with the shafts replaced in 1732 (JM 112). His mark has been recorded on no fewer than eleven pairs of *rimmonim*. Unlike de Oliveyra, who appears to have been born in Amsterdam in 1657 and moved to London in 1697, the other great maker of these ritual objects at this period was a gentile, William Spackman. Without the aid of hallmarks, it is virtually impossible to distinguish particularly the latter's *rimmonim* from slightly earlier Dutch examples (JM 113). Indeed, it may be that, rather than copying Dutch originals, Spackman imported them and then had them hallmarked in London prior to resale, as he would have been required to do by law.

Perhaps as a result of these similarities of design, it has been claimed by J. Stone in his 1965 *Quest* article 'English Silver *Rimmonim* and their Makers' that 'throughout the eighteenth century … English goldsmiths, of whom only two or three who made *rimmonim* were Jewish, took what for many of them was an unusually timid attitude towards the difficulty [of artistic originality]; and even where they did not copy existing *rimmonim*, they were inevitably strongly influenced by them. Yet this is not surprising. The problem faced by a Gentile goldsmith was to fulfil his patron's commission; unless he copied an existing pair of *rimmonim*, how could he, without knowledge of Jewish ritual and custom, be certain that he was correctly interpreting that commission? It was undoubtedly safer to copy; but, this safety-first attitude was destined to – and did in fact – stifle originality and inventiveness.'

*Opposite:*
**TORAH SCROLLS**
Charles Frederick Kandler, London,
1766–67
Silver, parchment
C 1992.2.1  395 x 140 mm (when closed);
C 1992.2.2  360 mm high
Miniature scrolls in silver cases, with pointers which act as securing pins when the scrolls are closed.
C 1992.2.1 & 2

*Above:*
***RIMMON***
Abraham de Oliveyra, London, 1716 (shafts 1732)
Silver-gilt, 515 mm high
*Rimmon* of open-bowl form, chased with foliage and flutes on matted ground, and with knurled rims and beaded scroll brackets. Octagonal gilt bells. Crown and flaming vase finial. Shaft lightly chased with flowers and false flutes. The earliest known example by this maker, eight years before his mark was registered.
JM 112

However, the examples by de Oliveyra appear to be generally more original than Spackman's, and this same inventiveness can be seen in many later English *rimmonim*. De Oliveyra's pair from 1716/32 (JM 112) and those of 1737 (JM 120) are of a quite distinctive form, which could perhaps be best described as incorporating an open bowl and cover with bells between. It is significant that an entry in the Bevis Marks records for 1737 states that de Oliveyra was given various pieces of silver for melting to offset the costs of making 'two pairs of little bells'.

This raises questions of artistic responsibility. This has been a long-running issue in the world of silver, indeed one that has plagued it since the late nineteenth-century Arts and Crafts movement helped to distort the picture by focusing so much attention on the individual silversmith. The so-called maker's mark in silver may indeed be that of the actual maker or of the person who imported a piece for sale. However, very often it is that of an individual who had registered a mark at Goldsmiths' Hall and who co-ordinated the work of other specialist casters, piercers, chasers, engravers and gilders. It may well be that de Oliveyra worked exactly in the latter role. He would have received the order from his co-religionists, who would have been involved in, at least, approving the design, and then de Oliveyra would have drawn together a team of craftsmen to work with him to meet the order, which would be struck with his 'maker's mark' on completion.

The Rococo style is well demonstrated by the decoration of two exceptional silver-mounted travelling Torah scrolls (C 1992.2.1 & 2). Made by the London goldsmith Charles Frederick Kandler in 1766 and 1767, their history is fascinating. The scrolls were made for Rabbi Hayim Samuel Jacob Falk, known as the *Ba'al Shem* of London. He has been described as a 'dabbler in magic, a maker of amulets and a kabbalist who used incantations to accomplish paranormal feats such as finding lost treasure'. Having been condemned to death in Westphalia as a sorcerer, Falk escaped and fled to London, where he arrived around 1742. He resisted attempts by the

**GEORGE III *RIMMONIM***
Hester Bateman, London, 1780
Silver
425 mm high
Vase-shaped bright-cut *rimmonim* made for the Great Synagogue in Portsmouth. Now in a private collection.
Copyright Christie's Images Ltd (1995)

**RIMMONIM**

England, *c.*1810
Silver
381 mm high
Formed as three graduated crowns with pierced bands surmounted by beaded arches with crosses *patté* and fleur-de-lis ornament. Finials formed as similar, smaller crowns. Shafts engraved with a commemorative Hebrew inscription.
JM 128

Ashkenazi community to persuade him to join their worship at the Great Synagogue. However, on his death in 1782 he left various bequests, including these scrolls, to that synagogue.

Kandler, the maker, is as interesting and elusive as the original owner of these scrolls. A great deal of research has been carried out into what now appear to be three distinct members of the family: Charles I, Charles II and the maker of these pieces, Charles Frederick. The latter seems to have taken over the business around 1735 and is recorded as dying of 'a fit of apoplexy at about 1 o'clock on the 15th of October, 1778'. There is extensive evidence that he was a Roman Catholic and was an active member of that community in St James's.

The scrolls Kandler provided for the *Ba'al Shem* of London vary slightly in their decoration, but they are beautifully designed with pure Rococo twisted, fluted baluster handles and finials. The plain accompanying silver pointers (*yadim*), which when not in use serve as pins to hold the double cases closed, are each enriched with a waved cuff to the hand and twisted finial. The miniature scrolls are mounted in an extraordinarily imaginative and stylistically up-to-date manner. It would be fascinating to know just how much input in their design the *Ba'al Shem* had; probably, given that this was clearly a 'one-off' order, it was very considerable.

A magnificent pair of vase-shaped, bright-cut, engraved *rimmonim* with bells hung from silver tassels, made for the Great Synagogue in Portsmouth by Hester Bateman in 1780, are equally innovative and exemplify the Neoclassical taste. Compare these *rimmonim* with a pair in the Jewish Museum collection, made around 1810 (JM 128), which also show an interesting and imaginative incorporation of Neoclassical ornament into these religious objects. While unmarked, it is possible that these are by Hester Bateman's son Peter and his nephew William Bateman, who made a pair with a somewhat similar pierced, bright-cut, engraved band in 1811. Although perhaps sacrilegious to say, it would be easy to imagine the bright-cut pierced bands on both these *rimmonim* forming the sides of secular wine coasters of the period.

# Ritual Silver in the Home

The artistic changes that can be seen in European eighteenth-century formal silver used in the synagogue also, of course, affected less grand objects made for use more usually in the home, such as the *Hanukah* lamp and spice box. The earliest recorded English *Hanukah* lamp is that by John Ruslen of 1709, made for Elias Lindo (JM 230). This has a backplate chased with the figure of Elijah, alluding to the original owner's first name. He is flanked by balanced scrolls, foliage and scale work and surmounted by a shell. It has been suggested that the rectangular drip tray beneath the lights may be a replacement, but the cartouche-shaped form of the backplate is a wonderful expression of late Baroque ornament and could well be that of a secular wall sconce of the period. It seems likely that the lamp was a wedding present to Elias, who married on 2 February

1709, at Bevis Marks, a synagogue for which the gentile silversmith who made this lamp worked for twenty-eight years.

The example by the specialist Frankfurt *Hanukah* lamp maker Rötger Herfurth, around 1740, is again a contrast in styles (JM 240). While the general outline remains balanced, the decoration of the lower skirt, the central chased urn and the *menorah* is all heavily Rococo in feel. Such Rococo decoration on *Hanukah* lamps and, indeed, in Judaica in general is found in Eastern Europe often well into the nineteenth century. More in keeping with European mainstream developments, although not made in a major centre, is the Neoclassical provincial German example made at the end of the eighteenth century, with its central ribbon and wreath cartouche flanked by urns (JM 244).

**HANUKAH LAMP**

John Ruslen, London, 1709
Silver
358 x 297 mm
Shaped backplate, repoussé and chased with a figure of Elijah and ravens, flanked by acanthus scrolls .
JM 230

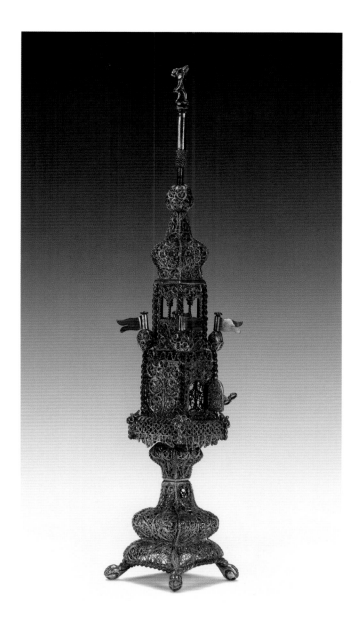

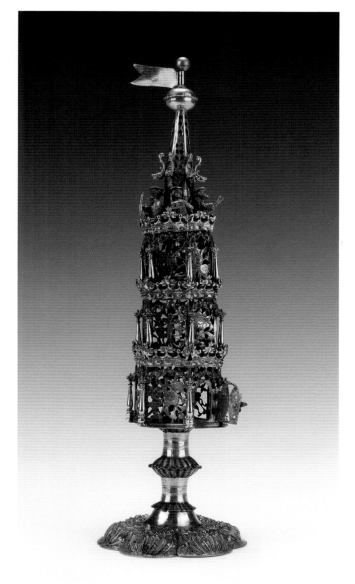

Spice boxes underwent the same stylistic changes as the eighteenth century advanced, although examples made in filigree are exceptionally conservative and difficult to date. Indeed, some have been tentatively said to be late seventeenth-century German but may well be Galician and of a much later date (for example JM 410). Unquestionably datable to the early eighteenth century is a fine example by the Berlin maker IAS, possibly Joachim Andreas Schaar (JM 412). The hexafoil foot chased with foliage and matting is absolutely typical of the period in Germany. More unusual are the six demi-figures of ritual workers from the synagogue, including the rabbi, butcher and beadle.

*Above left:*
**SPICE TOWER**
Germany, late seventeenth century (?)
Silver
292 mm high
Filigree square-section two-tiered turret on a square foot, with gilt claw feet. Flags at the angles of the lower tier. Shaped dome with ball and lion 'flag', with small figure above.
JM 410

*Above right:*
**SPICE TOWER**
Possibly by Joachim Andreas Schaar, Berlin, *c*.1700
Silver
348 mm high
Hexagonal three-tiered turret with pierced floral panels and angle columns, and with coronet galleries, the upper with six demi-figures of synagogue functionaries – a rabbi, a *shochet* (ritual butcher), a beadle, a *hazan* (reader) and two others, unidentified. Pierced steeple with dolphin crochets and ball-and-flag finial. Maker's mark: 'IAS'.
JM 412

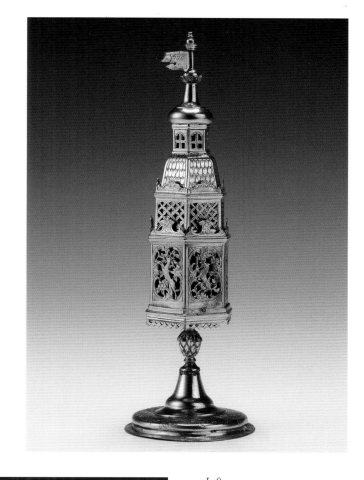

*Right:*
**SPICE TOWER**

Germany or Eastern Europe,
mid- to late eighteenth century
Silver
298 mm high
Hexagonal two-tiered turret on
circular foot with chased flowers
and pineapple stem; lower tier
pierced and engraved with
Rococo panels of animals and
birds and with gilt cresting,
upper tier with trellis-work
panels; tiled domed roof with
windowed cupola and flag finial.
Cyrillic mark and number '12'.
JM 420

A filigree example that is easily datable to the mid-eighteenth century, although of traditional tower form, is one that is inset with beautiful enamel panels, painted with Rococo landscapes and Old Testament scenes (JM 414). A number of other German mid-eighteenth-century examples incorporate Rococo decoration within the traditional architectural form (JM 420). A slightly later Berlin example is pierced with balanced wreaths and swirling paterae in the Neoclassical taste beneath a scale-work steeple (JM 421a).

*Opposite:*
**SPICE TOWER**

Schwäbisch Gmünd,
mid-eighteenth century
Silver, paste stones, enamel
255 mm high
Square filigree two-tiered turret
on shaped foot, studded with
coloured paste stones and
decorated with enamel plaques,
on lower tier with landscapes
and on upper tier with
miniatures of David, Abraham
preparing to sacrifice Isaac,
Jacob dreaming of his ladder,
and a fourth unidentified.
JM 414

*Left:*
**SPICE TOWER**

Berlin, late eighteenth century
Silver
262 mm
Hexagonal two-tiered turret,
with pierced panels chased with
laurel wreaths. Tall steeple
with ball finial. Polygonal foot,
chased with foliage.
JM 421a

# Evolution in Styles and Uses

Certain objects, however, remain functional and traditional with little or no regard for contemporary decoration. The beautiful sanctuary lamp by Abraham de Oliveyra (JM 373) is a case in point. Occasionally, individual objects such as the laver and ewer by Abraham Portal, London, from 1768 (JM 192), are stylistically wildly out of date. The basin and foot of this ewer are exceptionally conservative. Indeed, the foot of the ewer is strongly reminiscent of that of an English chalice of around 1700. Only its triple scroll handle has a real Rococo feel about it. That Portal could work in the latest fashion is amply demonstrated by a sophisticated silver-gilt ewer and basin that he made in 1756, engraved with the royal arms of George II and presented to Sir Charles Hanbury Williams on his appointment as ambassador to St Petersburg.

*Above:*
**LAVER AND EWER**
Abraham Portal, London, 1768
Silver  407 x 317 mm
Laver of plain circular basin form with narrow gadrooned rim. Helmet-shaped ewer on circular gadrooned foot, with corded rib around body, rising scroll handle capped with a leaf, and gadrooned rim with shell below lip. Engraved with the inscription 'New Synagogue Leadenhall Street'.
JM 192

*Left:*
**GEORGE II EWER AND BASIN**
Abraham Portal, London, 1756
Silver-gilt
Basin 407 x 585 mm
Copyright Christie's Images Ltd

*Right:*
**KIDDUSH CUPS**

Johan Adam Boller, Frankfurt, 1715
Silver
216 x 154 mm
Pair of beakers, originally presented to the Public Hospital of the Judengasse in Frankfurt in 1717, by Hirsch Oppenheim, for *kiddush* during the circumcision ceremony.
C 1978.7.31.1 & 1a

*Below:*
**COVERED BEAKER**

Joachim Christoph Schönermarck (?), Berlin, *c.*1735
Silver, gilt
330 x 165 mm
Bowl and lid are chased with arabesque strapwork and inset with two-thirds *thaler* and one-sixth *thaler* coins. Base and lid are inset with medals. Maker's mark: 'Schenermarck'.
C 1978.7.31.2

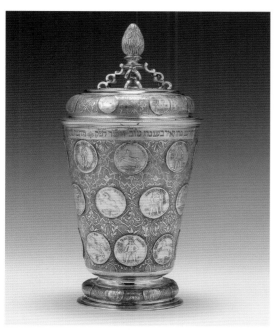

Apart from the creation of specialised functional objects for religious purposes, we also find examples of quite standard secular forms transformed into objects of great beauty and religious significance. A superb pair of engraved Frankfurt beakers, used for *kiddush* during the circumcision ceremony, were made by Johann Adam Boller, around 1715, in a form that is absolutely typical of that city (C 1978.7.31.1 & 1a). They are brought alive by the beautiful engraving, entirely covering the feet and sides, of laurel wreaths containing Hebrew inscriptions and the badges of the charity treasurers of the Jewish community from 1690 to 1769. A third fine German covered beaker, equally large and imposing, underlines the point. Set with coins within engraved strapwork, this beaker is a perfect example of a well-known Berlin secular type (C 1978.7.31.2). Probably made by Joachim Christoph Schönermarck around 1735, it is engraved with a slightly later Hebrew presentation inscription to the Chief Rabbi of Berlin, Hirschel Levin, dated 5533 (1773).

**LORD MAYOR'S SALVER**
John Ruslen, London, 1702
Silver
588 x 490 mm
Dish with the emblem of the
London Spanish and Portuguese
Synagogue in the centre. One
of the gifts presented annually
by Bevis Marks Synagogue to
the Lord Mayor of London from
1679 to 1778.
JM 656

In the same way, we find a standard oval tray, transformed by its special decoration to meet the purposes for which it was ordered (JM 656). This tray, made, like the *Hanukah* lamp, by John Ruslen (JM 230), dates from 1702. The basic form, with rich and elaborate repoussé and chased decoration in high relief, is similar to that found in the late 1660s and 1670s on two-handled trays, particularly those by another London maker, Jacob Bodendick. Its most distinctive feature is the central panel of Abraham by his tent with the inscription 'the arms of the Tribe of Judah, given them by the Lord', alluding to the badge of the Spanish and Portuguese Jewish congregation in London. By 1679 it had become customary for the Sephardi community of Bevis Marks Synagogue to present an annual gift of £50, or just such a silver dish heaped high with sweets, to the Lord Mayor of London. What is really very remarkable about this dish is its documentation. We know from the records of Bevis Marks that it cost the community a total of £33 16s. 6d., of which £1 10s. 6d. was 'for gift to the official of My Lord' (Mayor) and a further £5 was for the sweetmeats.

Five such trays by Ruslen are extant, of which the last is dated 1710, but examples by other makers are known. This form was succeeded by that of a standard early Georgian salver on feet, the centre with a finely engraved badge of Judah. A fine example of this, by Joseph Sanders, from 1737, was last recorded in a private American collection. The tray and then, in turn, the salver were replaced fairly shortly afterward by a two-handled cup. An example of the latter is one made by George Boothby in 1745. On a swirling fluted Rococo foot, the body is chased with Britannia holding a shield engraved with the arms of Judah (JM 657). In some ways the design of this Rococo cup, particularly the tree trunk handles, is somewhat inelegant. More satisfactory is a cup and cover of 1777 by Thomas and Richard Payne (JM 658). This, the very last of these silver presentations by the Sephardi community, is a perfect expression of 'Adamesque' Neoclassical silver, with its urn form, beaded scroll handles and drapery swags.

Although the Lord Mayor's tray and two cups were all made in London, they reflect the stylistic changes that can be seen in Judaica made throughout Europe in the 150 years from 1650. The great artistic movements that swept across Europe in this period are manifested throughout the rich and varied collection of the Jewish Museum, be it in the objects discussed here or any of the host of breast-plates, Torah crowns, *yadim*, *Megillah* cases, *etrog* boxes and *kiddush* cups. Ritual silver is almost by definition conservative. However, the silver objects in the collection brilliantly demonstrate the ability of European silversmiths to incorporate contemporary artistic design in their production of functional ritual objects. At its most successful this blend has resulted in objects of the greatest rarity and spectacular beauty.

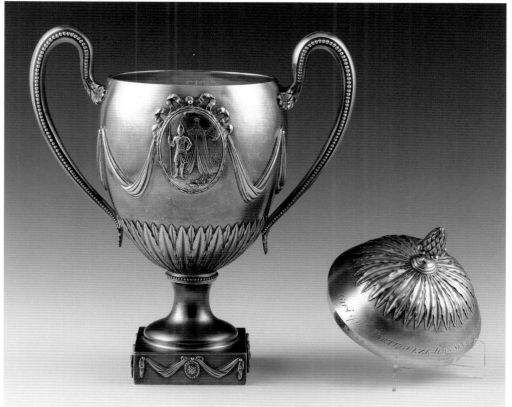

*Above:*
**LORD MAYOR'S CUP**
George Boothby, London, 1745
Silver
392 mm high
Cup decorated with applied emblematic figures of London and the Thames, adapted from the Mansion House pediment, and a seated Britannia with shield engraved with the arms of Judah. Presented by the congregation of Bevis Marks to Sir Richard Hoare, Lord Mayor of London 1745–46.
JM 657

*Left:*
**LORD MAYOR'S CUP**
Thomas and Richard Payne, London, 1777
Silver, gold
349 mm high
Cup decorated with the badge of Bevis Marks Synagogue. This was the last in the series of annual gifts given by Bevis Marks to the Lord Mayor of London, and was presented to Sir James Esdaile, Lord Mayor of London 1777–78.
JM 658

# FABRICS OF JEWISH LIFE

Jennifer Wearden

Textiles are often taken for granted, associated in the mind
with garments or furnishings. The efforts and skills involved in
the production of raw materials and the finished object are
rarely perceived. The fibres, dyes and specialised threads are
not obvious to the eye. In an age of cheap, mass-produced
fabric, the result of the Industrial Revolution, it is hard to
understand that textiles were once very expensive and
precious. Not only were they valued in themselves, but they
were used as coverings for other cherished possessions.
Textiles are flexible and can be folded, draped and sewn to
form almost any required shape. They can be easily laundered,
and also decorated.

Like the blank canvas on which an artist paints a picture, textiles are the ground fabric on which a pattern is printed or embroidered. They are versatile in that they can be woven and stitched with a variety of textures and can be decorated with braids, tassels and beads. However, textiles are particularly vulnerable to wear and tear and to damage by insects and bright light. Deterioration means that clothes are sometimes cut down and remodelled for children, and household fabrics are recycled as dusters and cleaning cloths. It is truly amazing that any textile survives intact for more than fifty years, and that fact alone means that they should occupy a special place in a museum collection.

Despite the fact that textiles are to be found in most public collections of decorative art, they are frequently underrated as 'works of art'. In the 1974 *Catalogue of the Jewish Museum* Natalie Rothstein discussed the historical importance of the Museum's textile collection, noting that although the collections in Prague or New York are more extensive, all the main types of textiles in terms of technique and function are represented in The Jewish Museum, London. They date from the mid-seventeenth century through to the twentieth century, and they vary in quality and in condition. Apart from the patterned silks, which were mostly woven in France, the majority of the fabrics found in this collection originated in northern Europe, made for Ashkenazi congregations, especially in Germany and the Low Countries. The practice of donating valuable woven silks and other fabrics from dresses and domestic textiles for synagogue use is well known, and this collection illustrates some of the most fashionable designs from the eighteenth century.

It may be surprising to learn that some of the most important textiles in this collection are not the highly coloured or patterned silks, but the plainer linings found on mantles and curtains. Because they are part of ritual objects, they have been cared for and are frequently in almost pristine condition, whereas linings used for everyday garments and furnishings have seldom survived intact, often being replaced when they became worn or heavily soiled. For a textile historian studying design, this collection is an important resource to be used in parallel with the vast textile collections in the Victoria & Albert Museum, and for a social or economic historian this collection is a potential source of inspiration.

# SYNAGOGUE TEXTILES

One of the most magnificent pieces in the collection is the Torah mantle (JM 62) from the Hambro Synagogue, dating from between 1720 and 1725. In keeping with its function, it is dignified and restrained. It is sometimes difficult to distinguish between the work of a professional embroiderer and that of a highly skilled amateur, but the quality of these embroidered panels is such that it is inconceivable that they are anything but the products of a specialised workshop. Metal threads are difficult to manipulate, especially when worked over padding to create solid, three-dimensional figures known as 'raised work'. The padding can be made from soft fibres of wool or silk, or it can be in the form of small blocks of wood; in the nineteenth and twentieth centuries metal thread was often worked over thin cardboard templates to give a slightly raised profile. The beauty of this embroidery is in the detail: the delicacy of the grapevine that winds around the pillars on the Ark of the Covenant depicted in the central panel, and the contrast between the fragile stems and the angular solidity of the ark, which is topped by two realistic and perfectly formed vases of flowers.

**TORAH MANTLE** (detail of an embroidered panel)
France (silk), Spain or Italy (embroidery), 1720–25
Silk, velvet, silver-gilt, silver wire
Blue silk mantle with three panels embroidered on a red velvet ground with metal thread in raised work. Each panel is decorated with an ark, each containing a different motif, with a panel of ornament above and below. From the Hambro Synagogue, London.
JM 62

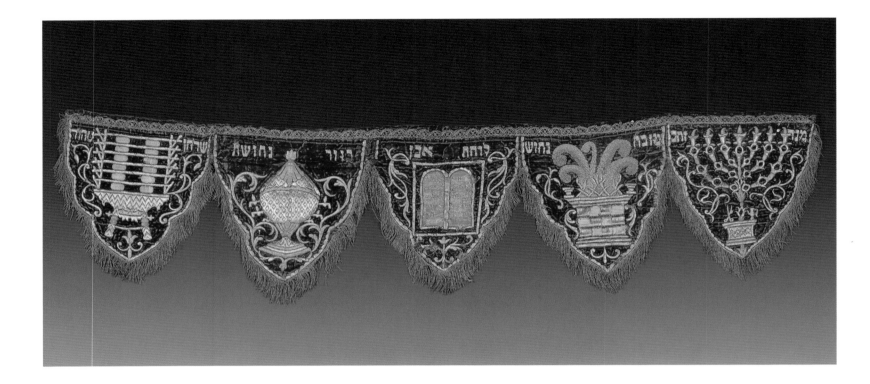

Great ceremonial textiles are often embroidered with metal thread. The shimmering silver and silver-gilt threads look magnificent, and the cost of commissioning such mantles reflects the respect accorded to the Torah scrolls they cover. In Europe and the Middle East professional metal thread embroidery has traditionally been worked by men because it was said that women's hands would tarnish the threads, and it is true that the skin of women's hands is more acidic at certain times in their menstrual cycle. A Torah mantle dated 1833 bears the arms of the Salomons family (JM 81; see p. 46). Sir David Salomons was the first Jewish Lord Mayor of London (1855–56), and his coat of arms can be found on several items in the Museum, including panels from his carriage doors (see p. 32). The Salomons mantle is fashionably dramatic, because the solid embroidery is set against a background of plain velvet, and is typical of the desire for simplicity in the late Georgian period, whereas the eighteenth-century mantle has a delicacy in keeping with the more frivolous style of its time. On the other hand, the designs on some ceremonial textiles give no clue to their date. The symbols on a late seventeenth- or early eighteenth-century pelmet (JM 34) are timeless, and only secondary characteristics, such as the quality of the velvet on which they are embroidered and the types of metal thread and stitches used, enable them to be dated.

*Above:*

**PELMET FOR ARK CURTAIN**

Place of origin unknown, late seventeenth or early eighteenth century
Velvet, linen, silver-gilt, silver thread, gold thread
0.28 x 1.38 m
Pelmet embroidered with raised gold and silver thread and silver-gilt sequins on a crimson velvet ground, with a plain white linen lining. Five panels, each with a scalloped edge and a gold fringe, contain sacred objects (table with loaves of Showbread, laver, Tablets of the Law, Altar, *Menorah*) and Hebrew inscriptions. A strip of silver-gilt lace is sewn to the upper edge.
JM 34

*Opposite:*

**PASSOVER CUSHION**

Place of origin unknown, eighteenth century
Silk, silk thread, silver thread
515 x 515 mm
Red silk cushion to enable the celebrant to carry out the commandment to eat the Passover meal reclining. Embroidered in silver thread, with central design in silks. Four tassels of silver thread. Central embroidered scene shows the High Priest about to sacrifice the paschal lamb, with the city of Jerusalem in the background.
JM 361

# PERSONAL AND DOMESTIC TEXTILES

Textiles used within the home rather than the synagogue, albeit in a ceremonial setting such as the Sabbath meal, often reflect the popular styles of the period in which they were made, and there is a greater probability that many were made by amateurs. One beautiful Passover cushion (JM 361) appears to be a combination of professional and amateur work, with the scrolling metal-thread embroidery emanating from a workshop and the coloured silk embroidery depicting Jerusalem, the High Priest and the sacrificial lamb being worked by another, less skilful hand. Both the pelmet and the cushion serve a functional purpose and did not require decoration, but symbols have been added to retell a familiar story and remind those who see them of important religious traditions. Many faiths use art to transmit their doctrines, to teach their congregations about basic truths, but this is not necessarily the case here. For Jewish people the stories of the Bible are read and interpreted in public worship, and the predominance of the word has historically led to a high rate of literacy, so it is unlikely that the images on these textiles were intended purely for educational purposes. They did, however, create a decorative background for both family and public worship and gave pleasure to those who saw them.

*Above:*
**MIZRACH**
Place of origin unknown,
nineteenth century
Velvet, coloured threads
256 x 313 mm
Petit-point embroidery on
velvet. Design of two lions and
*Magen David* (Star of David).
JM 9

*Below:*
**PORTRAIT OF RABBI AKIVA EGER
THE YOUNGER (1761–1837)**
Place of origin unknown,
nineteenth century
Canvas, coloured threads
525 x 440 mm
Framed and glazed needlework
portrait.
JM 859

Since the early years of the nineteenth century the combination of woven canvas, coloured woollen or silk threads and a printed chart has been used to make popular embroidery kits which could be bought and worked at home. A portrait of Rabbi Akiva Eger the Younger (1761–1837) is a superb example (JM 859). A printed paper chart would have indicated which colour, thickness of thread and type of stitch was to be used, but as anyone who has tried to follow a modern embroidery kit will know, great skill would have been required to achieve the exceptionally fine details of the face and beard. Although the *mizrach* (the plaque placed on the eastern wall to show the direction of prayer) worked entirely in cross stitch on velvet (JM 9) would also have been copied from a printed chart and is far simpler than the portrait, its simplicity is deceptive. It is not possible to work a detailed and subtly shaded cross-stitch design directly on velvet because the soft pile of the velvet obscures the woven threads which have to be counted to make the even embroidery stitches. Cross stitch is worked by taking the embroidery yarn diagonally over an even number of threads in the woven ground fabric. A canvas is ideal because it is easy to see and count these interlacing threads. The only way to work on velvet would be to stitch a piece of canvas on top of the velvet and embroider through both layers – canvas and velvet – and, when it is finished, carefully to cut away and pull out every bit of unworked canvas. Technically this is not difficult, but it requires care and patience, and surprising strength because velvet is a tightly woven fabric and it is not easy to slip a needle in and out of it. For these reasons it is possible that this example was produced in a professional workshop. Had it been worked on ordinary canvas, it could easily have been done by an amateur embroiderer.

In a museum setting, especially in a collection that includes magnificent works of art in precious metals or exquisite manuscripts, the word 'amateur' might imply 'less important', but this is never the case here. An example created in the home, such as the *arba kanfot* (fringed garment) made in the 1920s by a lady for her grandson (C 1998.5), was made not only with love for him but also with the hope that he would grow up within Jewish tradition. If a woman lacked the skills to create

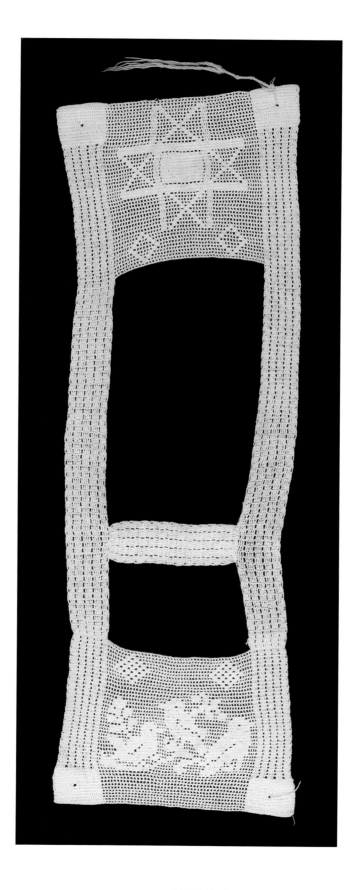

**ARBA KANFOT**
Mrs M. Abrahams, England, 1920s
Linen (?)  *c.* 600 mm long
Crocheted child's *arba kanfot*, with
a *Magen David* and bird design.
C 1998.5

an item herself, a piece of material previously used for a secular function could be donated for use in a religious context. Pieces of expensive silk, probably taken from a once fashionable embroidered apron, were re-made into a Torah mantle (JM 68), and many other examples exist in this collection of textiles recycled from garments and transformed into covers and curtains for use in the synagogue. Some were expensive, such as the silks used in one curtain probably made up in the late

eighteenth century (JM 32), while others, such as those used in the cover made in the early nineteenth century for a reading desk (JM 97), were from poorer fabrics. Mundane items such as these 'poorer fabrics' or the crocheted *arba kanfot* seldom survive, but when they do, because of their relative rarity, they are invaluable to anyone interested in textile history or social history; and because they are 'ordinary' it is often easier for us to relate to them in a personal way than to great works of decorative art.

# Textiles with Different Meanings

The *tallit* or *tefillin* bags (JM 181 and JM 182) are examples of 'mass-produced' textiles in this collection that permit us to glimpse the wider commercial context in which textiles were manufactured. Travellers to Arab North Africa in the eighteenth century often commissioned local craftsmen to customise useful items such as fine leather or velvet wallets and purses by adding their name, the date and occasionally their address to the embroidered decoration. Tunis and Algiers were noted centres for this trade in souvenirs. It appears to have worked in much the same way that a modern visitor to Hong Kong can be measured for a suit and collect it from the tailor a few days later: in the eighteenth century a customer would select a wallet or bag and have an inscription of their own devising embroidered into the fabric. Such personalised souvenirs would have been exciting gifts to receive, and the great advantages of giving textiles are that they are generally functional and easy to transport.

*Above:*
### BIMAH COVER
Place of origin unknown, early nineteenth century
Silk, velveteen, flannel, cotton, linen, metal thread
560 x 530 mm
Cloth for synagogue reading desk, made from several different materials. From centre to outer square these are: brocaded silk fragment edged with metal strip; crimson silk damask; green velveteen; red flannel; buff flannel; black velveteen; blue, buff and green cotton. Traces of pale blue silk on the sides, and rosettes in metal thread on blue flannel on the corners between the red and buff flannels. Lined with blue and brown linen.
JM 97

*Left:*
### TALLIT BAG
Gibraltar, 1786
Velvet, canvas, gold thread, cord
257 x 259 mm
Green velvet bag with red and green striped tassels and cords, and lining of white canvas. Embroidered in gold thread with inscriptions giving the owner's name in Hebrew and Roman characters, and a stylised floral pattern.
JM 182

Souvenir printed cotton handkerchiefs were extremely popular from the late eighteenth century until the middle of the twentieth, when the use of paper tissues made the washable version virtually obsolete. Large cotton handkerchiefs often served as vehicles for political comment, as mementoes of important events, such as international exhibitions, coronations and battles, or as celebrations of the lives of influential people. The handkerchief depicting Prussian Jewish soldiers observing the Day of Atonement in an army camp at Metz during the Franco-Prussian War (1870–71; Metz was taken by the Prussians in October 1870) is an excellent example of textile printing from an engraved copper plate (JM 664).

Probably the most intriguing textile in this collection is the beautiful eighteenth-century embroidered ark curtain (JM 44). It was made in a workshop somewhere in the Ottoman Empire and, like the embroidered bags and the printed handkerchief, this large hanging may well have been made for an international, rather than a local, market. It may have been made in Istanbul or in one of the larger towns of what is now Turkey, but another possibility is that it was made in Banja Luka in Bosnia, which was part of the Ottoman Empire in Europe and which was noted for the production of similar fine pieces. The group of buildings in the centre, with its six minarets, probably represents the complex of Sultan Ahmet in Istanbul. This single textile could inspire a series of debates about the interpretation of pattern, the importance of symbolism, and the relationship between function and design. The centrepiece indicates a Muslim context, but all the other devices on the curtain are archetypal Jewish symbols, making this a fascinating blend of Jewish and Ottoman iconographies.

Textiles can serve as powerful statements of identity, and there are several banners in the collection that proclaim not only the name of a group of people but also the values for which they stand. The painted silk banner of the Jews' Orphan Asylum dated 1831 (1989.115; see p.11), an embroidered velvet union leader's sash made by Toye & Co. in the early twentieth century (1992.26.3) and the painted silk banner of the Jewish Bakers' Union from the 1920s (1984.126) take us away from the ceremonial use of textiles in the synagogue, the ritual use of textiles in the home and the personal use of textiles by individuals into the realm of London social and political life. Flag-waving, banner-carrying – these are public, dynamic activities and intended to promote changes in society. The complexity of textiles reflects their myriad uses. Only imagination and individual skill limit the ways they can be shaped and decorated.

*Left:*

**PRESIDENT'S SASH, LONDON JEWISH BAKERS' UNION (LJBU)**
Toye & Co., London, early twentieth century
Velvet, cotton, silk, paper, braid
0.15 x 2 m
Red velvet sash decorated with gold fringe and tassels, embroidered gold lettering and white appliqué LJBU label. Formed in 1905, the LJBU campaigned to improve the conditions of Jewish bakers in the East End. To encourage customers to buy only 'union bread', every loaf from an organised shop carried a paper label similar to the one depicted on the sash.
1992.26.3

*Opposite:*

**LONDON JEWISH BAKERS' UNION (LJBU) BANNER**
London, 1920s
Silk, paint, wood, wool
Banner 2.33 x 2.08 m;
fringes 90 mm long;
tabs each 95 x 50 mm
Banner with union slogans in English on one side and Yiddish on the other.
1984.126
*(Front)* A central panel contains figures of two bakers, with a union label between them, and two loaves of bread carrying union labels at their feet. At each side of the central panel are ears of wheat bound by banners carrying LJBU and general trade union slogans.
*(Reverse)* A central panel containing four arms pointing to a union label, surrounded by banners carrying trade union slogans in Yiddish.

# FROM CRADLE TO GRAVE

## THE JEWISH LIFE CYCLE

Shalom Sabar

Objects play an important role in the performance of rituals.
Together with special costumes, foods, customs and the
recitation of blessings or songs they stimulate our senses
and make the ritual memorable and precious. Moreover,
they engender a sense of community among the participants,
leaving indelible impressions of belonging and shared
experience. Thus the carefully made ceremonial objects,
whose form and function are passed on from one generation
to another, create a strong bond with the ritual that long
outlasts the ceremony itself.

In the Jewish tradition objects seem to be secondary. The tangible realm is subordinated to the spiritual one. Yet almost no ceremony in the Jewish life cycle can be imagined without the use of appropriate objects. Early on the rabbis used the terms *hibbuv mitzvah* ('love of the commandment') and *hiddur mitzvah* ('beautification or embellishment of the commandment') to stress the concept that the service of the Lord should be performed in a pleasant atmosphere with beautiful objects. The blessing over aromatic spices at the *Havdalah* ceremony that marks the close of the Sabbath does not require any object, but putting the spices in a costly and richly ornamented silver box fulfils the concept of *hiddur mitzvah*.

In traditional societies the life cycle is generally divided into four stages, each accompanied by a series of rituals. The four stages and the events associated with them in Jewish tradition comprise the following:

- Childbirth and early childhood (circumcision, redemption of the first-born, etc.)
- Coming of age or initiation (*Barmitzvah* or *Batmitzvah*)
- Marriage (*kiddushin* and *nissu'in*)
- Death, burial and mourning

The rituals performed in these ceremonies are known as 'rites of passage', and the objects used in them can be considered 'transitional objects', symbolic of the changes in life. In the case of Jewish objects their design and decoration also reflect adaptation to the host culture, whether in Christian Europe or the Islamic East.

# CHILDBIRTH AND CHILDHOOD

Most rites of passage are accompanied by anxieties and worries, which provide the motivation underlying folk beliefs in the power of sympathetic magic. This is especially true of childbirth. The high infant mortality rate and dangers to the mother during labour in the pre-modern world fuelled the vast production of amulets and other protective talismans and conjurations. In this the Jews were no different from any other traditional society. However, Jewish amulets are characterised mainly by their Hebrew inscriptions and by their contents, which, despite objections raised at times by rabbinical authorities, have been derived from traditional sources. The midrashic figure of Lilith, supposedly Adam's first wife, rejected by him because of her assertiveness, is held responsible for the death of babies during childbirth. When her demands for equal rights were turned down, she decided to take revenge on the babies born to Adam and Eve and their descendants. The legend holds that three mysterious angels, Sanoi (or Sanvai), Sansanoi (or Sansavai) and Semanglof, made a contract with her not to harm the mother or her baby if she saw their names written or their image drawn in the houses she visited. (The legend appears fully for the first time in the Hebrew anthology of legends Alfa Beta de-Ben Sira, probably composed in Babylonia around the tenth century CE.)

The names of the three angels are beautifully embroidered on a Baghdadi amulet in the Jewish Museum's collection, which was apparently hung in the room where a baby was born (C 1974.1.7.2). The inscription opens with the powerful name of the Almighty, *Shaddai*, and, following the names of the angels, the words *hutz Lilith* appear – that is, 'Lilith begone'. An additional protective measure is the triangular shape of the amulet, for it is commonly believed that the tapering shape has the power to reduce evil forces. Sharing the beliefs of their

**AMULET**
Morocco (?), date unknown
Silver
32 mm high
Amulet in the shape of a hand
(*hamsa*), engraved with the
Hebrew name of God on the
palm and with sprigs of foliage
on the fingers.
JM 599

*Left:*
**AMULET**
Italy, *c.*1680
Silver, gilt
122 mm high
Amulet for a newborn baby,
with decoration in the form of
scrolls, Hebrew inscriptions and
symbolic objects on both sides.
JM 594

Muslim neighbours, the Jews of the lands of Islam employed two other important protective designs: the fish and the hand (*hamsa*). These elements were entirely 'Judaised' and understood as genuine Jewish symbols. The Hebrew letter *he*, representing the magical number five as well as the name of God, is often centrally inscribed on metal Jewish *hamsas*, and the five fingers are frequently spread, as in *Birkat Kohanim* ('Priestly Benediction', Numbers 6:24–26). The fish has become a symbol of good luck and fertility by virtue of the blessing given at its creation on the fifth day to 'be fruitful and multiply' (Genesis 1:22), as well as several other ideas expressed in the Talmud.

*Left and below:*
**MEZUZOT**
Caucasus, late nineteenth
century
Metal, niello
Two nielloed *mezuzot* in the
shape of fish.
C 1996.2.7

*Left:*
**AMULET**
Morocco (?), nineteenth century (?)
Silver
108 mm long
Hexagonal case chased with bands
of inscription mentioning the angels
Gabriel, Michael and (N)uriel, and
hung with medallions on chains.
JM 611

*Below:*
**AMULET**
Baghdadi, nineteenth century
Velvet, linen, gold thread, silver
thread
412 x 483 mm
Embroidered amulet for
protection against the Evil Eye
during childbirth.
C 1974.1.7.2

In the lands of Islam the use of protective amulets
continued throughout childhood. Both boys and girls wore
amulets, which often doubled as decorative pieces of jewellery.
For instance, a hexagonal belt pendant for boys is engraved
with the omnipotent forty-two-letter name of God (JM 611).
While the Jews of Europe by and large preferred paper
amulets, used mostly in the days before and after childbirth,
Italian Jews created attractive silver cases for their amulets.
Called *Shaddai*, this type of elaborate case (JM 594), which
was usually produced by Christian silversmiths, clearly reflects
in general design and ornamentation the influence of
contemporary Italian decorative arts. The main symbolic
elements are gilt appliqués depicting the holy implements of
the Temple: Tablets of the Law, Golden Altar, Levite Harp,
*menorah*, and the censer and mitre of the High Priest. Italian
Jews believed that the sacredness associated with these
symbols kept the newborn safe.

*Right:*

**CIRCUMCISION SET**

London (powder bottle from Netherlands), *c.*1844
Rosewood, silver, glass, velvet, brass
Case 276 mm wide
Circumcision set in a rosewood case, with silver plaque on lid, engraved with a dedicatory inscription in Hebrew. Contains two engraved circular dishes, two shields with London hallmark of 1844, knife with two detached blades, small oblong powder bottle, small egg-shaped box, two glass bottles with plated stoppers, two plated dishes with gadrooned rims. (Pair of scissors missing.)
JM 499

*Below:*

**CIRCUMCISION SET**

Salonika (or North Africa?), eighteenth century
Silver, silver-gilt, agate, velvet
Octagonal casket for circumcision set, chased with panels of foliage and dedicatory Hebrew inscriptions. Contains two chased shields, also inscribed, an octagonal powder box and an agate-handled knife.
JM 500

While the amulets constituted a popular reaction to the dangers of daily life, the circumcision ceremony on the eighth day is a mandatory ritual dating back to biblical times. Symbolising the covenant between God and Abraham and the promise that his seed would inherit the land, it is through this ceremony that the male child 'enters the covenant' and becomes a full Jew. This commandment has an obvious role in establishing a defining characteristic of Jews compared with other groups. It is clear, therefore, that the objects produced for this ceremony were not viewed simply as tools for a physical purpose. Rather, the circumcision knife and shield, or the special double cup used by German Jews, were often made of costly materials by expert silversmiths, who sought to design attractive ritual implements, fitting the transitional and irreversible nature of the ceremony (JM 500). Moreover, in many places they were kept in a specially crafted case, which the *mohel* (circumciser) proudly carried with him from one ceremony to the next (JM 499). The esteemed position of the *mohel* is reflected in another popular item, common especially in Ashkenazi communities: the *Mohelbuch* ('mohelbook'), a manuscript, at times individually commissioned, of relevant texts, such as the circumcision liturgy and its customs and laws, which also included blank pages where the *mohel* would list all the babies he circumcised (JM 641). Many *mohel* books were enhanced by colour illustrations, which shed light on the circumcision customs of bygone ages.

In German-speaking lands even the swaddling cloth used during the circumcision became a sacred object, later dedicated to the synagogue and used as a Torah binder. The Jewish Museum has a large collection of these binders, known in Hebrew as *mappah*, or in German as *wimpel*. Following the circumcision ceremony, the cloth was cleaned and cut into three or four pieces, which were stitched together to form a long strip of linen. The *wimpel* was then embroidered (and, from about 1750, painted) with a lengthy inscription, opening with the name of the child, the name of his father and the full Hebrew date of his birth. This is followed by a blessing taken from the circumcision liturgy, which delineates the ideal development of a Jewish child: 'May he grow to [the study of] Torah, to get married [*huppah*], and to perform good deeds.

**MOHEL** BOOK

Unknown member of Canstatt family, Germany, *c.*1788
Paper, leather
155 x 105 mm
Register compiled by two, possibly three, different *mohelim*, comprising forty-eight paper leaves written in German script, with ink-and-wash drawings. Leather gold-tooled binding with the original owner's name, Jacob Canstatt, impressed on the front. Canstatt used it just four times, between 1788 and 1792, all in Mannheim. The second *mohel* (name unknown) reversed the book and used it back to front from 28 *Ab* 5543 (1823), recording ten cases in Sheerness, eighteen in Chatham and one in Dover. The last entry was made on 22 *Heshvan* 1851.
JM 641

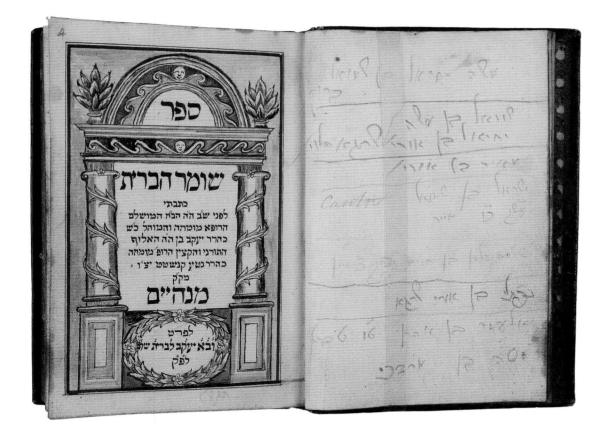

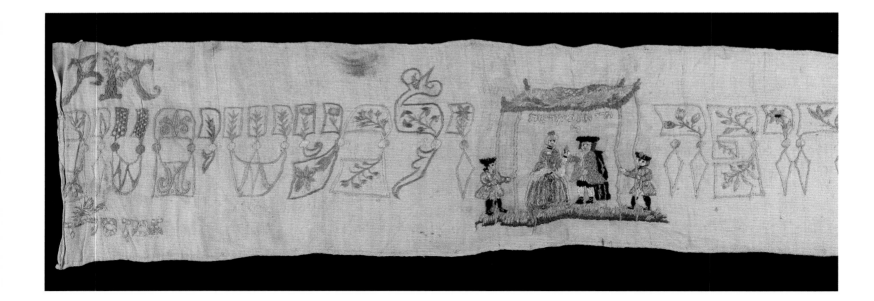

Amen, Selah.' These words were often embroidered with appropriate imagery. Thus, for example, for birth there is mainly the zodiacal sign of the month in which the baby was born; for *Barmitzvah*, scenes related to the reading of the Torah scroll in the synagogue; for the wedding, a wide range of marriage scenes reflecting the wedding customs and costumes current among German Jewry at the time. The beautifully decorated *wimpel* was then dedicated in a moving ceremony as a Torah binder upon the child's first visit to the synagogue (*Schuletragen*). Thus, the circumcision cloth – the symbol of the child's first bond with his people and community – now symbolically 'tied' him to the Torah. Moreover, upon his *Barmitzvah* he would read from the scroll tied with his personal binder.

Besides the baby and the *mohel*, two other important figures in the ceremony are the *sandak* (godfather) and the prophet Elijah, who is believed to attend every circumcision ceremony, to see for himself that the Israelites have not forsaken God's covenant (I Kings 19:14) – taken by the rabbis to mean circumcision. An elaborate Elijah chair is therefore prepared, symbolically showing his presence at the ceremony. Various customs concerning the size, shape and ornamentation of the chair developed over the ages. The attractive mahogany Elijah chair from the London Great Synagogue presents the tradition common among the Ashkenazim in the last centuries: a bench divided into two seats, one (usually the left) for the *sandak*, the other remaining empty for Elijah (JM 503). Among some Sephardi communities and Jews of the lands of Islam the night before circumcision, perceived as a time of danger and vulnerability, is named after the prophet. So too are special objects, in particular 'Elijah's Tray' – a tray of many candles brought to the room of the newborn.

*Above:*
**TORAH BINDER** (detail)
Bavaria or Austria, *c.*1762
Linen, silk thread, silver thread
0.17 x 2.18 m
Incomplete linen binder embroidered in coloured silks and silver thread. Letters embroidered with various flowers; above the date, a double Austrian eagle holding sceptres and orb. A wedding scene is also depicted.
JM 533

*Above:*

**TORAH BINDER** (detail)

Bavaria, *c.*1852

Painted linen

0.18 x 3.08 m

Linen binder with hand-painted patterned letters. Many vignettes, including a marriage scene and a man holding Torah scrolls. Margins decorated with birds and animals.

JM 567

*Right:*

**ELIJAH CHAIR**

England, 1809

Mahogany, brass, cloth, silver thread

1.22 x 1.22 m

High double chair for use at the circumcision ceremony. The back with a pediment inset with a brass plaque, bearing a Hebrew inscription identifying the original donor. Two cushions embroidered in silver thread with inscriptions relating to the ceremony and, on the right, hands raised in priestly blessing. The godfather sat on the left, and the seat on the right was reserved for Elijah. From the Great Synagogue, London.

JM 503

**BARMITZVAH ROBE**
Samarkand, *c.*1915
Velvet, silk, cotton, braid
Bukharan *Barmitzvah* robe.
Black velvet on blue silk, lined
with floral cotton, and with red
and green braid edging.
C 2004.4

It is perhaps not surprising that only a handful of objects related to the *Barmitzvah* ceremony are preserved, since this ritual, so common nowadays, is a relative newcomer in the Jewish tradition. It developed among the Jews of Germany in the Middle Ages, spread to other Ashkenazi and Italian communities, but was little known among the Sephardim or in the lands of Islam until recent times. In fact, in Yemen and some other places no special ceremony celebrated the first time a child read from the Torah, which took place years before his thirteenth birthday, and reaching that age had no ritualistic significance whatsoever. An exceptional item in the Museum's collection is a ceremonial robe, especially prepared for a *Barmitzvah* boy in one of the Bukharan communities of Uzbekistan, in the typical splendid manner of colourful brocade embroidery known from this region (C 2004.4).

# THE WEDDING

While the preparations for the circumcision ceremony had to be made quickly, the wedding was carefully planned and prepared, sometimes many years in advance. The importance of marriage and its status in the Jewish life cycle are implied by the Hebrew term for marriage, *kiddushin*, derived from a root meaning 'to be holy'. Jewish tradition celebrates marriage. The world was created for procreation, and every man is obliged to take a wife in order to fulfil this commandment.

The wedding is therefore considered the most joyous and spectacular event in one's life, and numerous objects are connected with its celebration. In addition to the required ceremonial objects, such as the *ketubah* (marriage contract), wedding ring and *huppah* (wedding canopy), there are the many articles of the dowry, the bridal trousseau and customary wedding gifts (known as *sivlonot*). Many works of art depict the Jewish wedding in various places and times. One such image is the painting by the noted Frankfurt Jewish artist Moritz Daniel Oppenheim (1800–1882), which was copied on a

marriage plate (JM 465). Oppenheim's picture provides a nostalgic view of a wedding in the Germany of his childhood, depicting bygone customs and objects – including the way in which elaborate wedding belts were worn around the waists of the bridal couple under the *huppah* (JM 453).

*Above:*
**MARRIAGE BELT**
Christian Mentzel I (?),
Germany, *c.*1670
Silver
972 mm long
Belt made up of twenty-seven links pierced and chased with rosettes and scrolls, fastened by a circular clasp with applied rosette.
JM 453

*Left:*
**MARRIAGE PLATE**
Germany, nineteenth century
Pewter
263 mm diameter
Plate with shaped beaded border. Centre embossed with a wedding scene in eighteenth-century dress; bride and bridegroom shown under the *huppah* (bridal canopy).
JM 465

**MARRIAGE RING**
Italy, fourteenth century
(hoop probably later)
Gold
37 mm high (including bezel)
Gold ring with plain hoop. Bezel
formed as an oblong Gothic
building with pierced arcaded
sides and gabled roof, engraved
in Hebrew, with ball finial.
JM 454

Especially prominent in the collection of the Jewish Museum are two important groups of wedding objects: marriage rings and *ketubot*. The rings, which are thought to date from the Gothic and Renaissance periods, can take two forms. One type, in gold, has a building as bezel symbolising both the Temple and the Jewish home; this probably dates from the fourteenth century (JM 454). Another type is a filigree hoop of slightly later date, probably the sixteenth or seventeenth century (JM 463). They originate in Germany and northern Italy, and often have the words *Mazal Tov* ('good luck') on them.

From a legal point of view the *ketubah* is far more important and was in use long before the ring. In Jewish law 'a man is not allowed to live with his wife, even for one single hour, without a *ketubah*'. Jewish marriage contracts from as early as the fifth century BCE have been discovered in the Jewish military colony of Elephantine, Egypt. The concept and basic form of the *ketubah* as it is known to us today were developed in Mishnaic and Talmudic times (first to sixth centuries CE); it aimed mainly to protect the legal rights of the woman and to make divorce difficult – the Bible permits the husband to divorce his wife at will. Originally the wording differed between Babylonia and Israel-Egypt, but the former gradually became the norm.

Decoration of the *ketubah* and the inclusion of items of the dowry became a way to broadcast the families' status. From a simple beginning in medieval Egypt and Israel new motifs and designs were added by Sephardi communities in Europe. One rabbinical authority (Simeon ben Zemah Duran of Majorca, 1361–1444) even recommended filling the borders of the document with designs as a safeguard against fraudulent additions to the text.

Following the expulsion of the Jews from the Iberian peninsula, the tradition of *ketubah* illustration was spread by the exiles and influenced local communities to follow suit. The earliest extant group of post-expulsion illustrated *ketubot* comes from the prominent Sephardi community of Venice, who also introduced the custom to the *tedeschi* (Ashkenazim) and other communities in the Venice Ghetto. An important example is the Venice 1624 *ketubah* in the Museum (JM 465a). The text is enclosed in a Moorish arch, familiar from medieval Spain. However, unlike Sephardi-Venetian *ketubot*, this contract does not include a *tena'im* (marital conditions) column, because the married parties were not Sephardim. It is clear therefore that by this year the Ashkenazim were imitating the Sephardi custom.

**MARRIAGE RING**
Italy, probably sixteenth to
seventeenth century
Gold, enamel
37 mm high (including bezel)
Filigree ring with large central
bosses and small border bosses
decorated with blue and white
enamel, and a blue enamel
gabled roof hinged to reveal a
small locket.
JM 463

# DEATH AND BURIAL

In contrast to the earlier stages in the life cycle, the end of life is marked by much solemnity and reverence. The rituals and customs of death, burial and *yahrzeit* (the anniversary of a death) are carefully planned to ease the plight of those who have lost a relative or a close friend. Great respect is given to the dying, and many customs have developed over the ages to mourn the dead and preserve their memory among the living.

Since Antiquity elaborate memorials and tombstones have been part of Jewish life in the land of Israel and elsewhere. The art of the Jewish tombstone continued in the Middle Ages, with significant differences between the various traditions and communities. The creation of holy burial societies (*Hevra Kadisha*) in sixteenth- to eighteenth-century Europe (modelled on the noted Prague society established by Rabbi Eleazar Ashkenazi in 1564) gave rise to the commissioning of many other ritualistic objects such as silver cups (C 1988.33).

In the course of the seventeenth and eighteenth centuries Italy became the foremost centre of *ketubah* illustration. Rich Italian families vied with each other over whose *ketubah* was more attractive; fine examples were proudly displayed at the wedding ceremony, and were personalised through the careful selection of popular biblical episodes and heroes bearing the same names as the bridal couple. In an example from Verona from 1678 (JM 467) two scenes from the life of David relate to David Montalcino, the bridegroom: David, composer of the Psalms and pious servant of the Lord, is shown playing his harp (top centre), juxtaposed with the heroic figure of young David slaying Goliath (bottom centre). In another most interesting *ketubah*, from the Adriatic coastal town of Senigallia, from 1805 (JM 479), only a scene for the bride is shown – King Ahasuerus handing Queen Esther the sceptre. This scene was carefully selected to honour the bride, Esther Morpurgo, a member of one of the most prominent and influential families in the history of Italian Jews.

*Left:*
***HEVRA KADISHA* CUP**
Silesia, 1875
Silver, metal
240 mm high without lid,
320 mm high with lid
Silver-plated cup and cover
with a commemorative
inscription in Hebrew and
German.
C 1988.33

Series of three *vanitas* paintings
Benjamin Senior Godines,
Amsterdam, 1679–81
Commissioned by Isaac de
Matatiah Aboab
Oil on parchment

*Left:*

**A MEMENTO MORI**
300 x 380 mm
A fashionably dressed young
man, attended by a servant,
starts on seeing bones and a
rotting corpse attacked by flies
and birds in a cemetery.
JM 895.1

Of great and unusual importance are three rare pictures related to death in the Museum's collection. They present a deep and thoughtful image of death – totally unfamiliar in its iconography and innovative approach within the realm of 'Jewish art'. These pictures are dated 1679 to 1681. The artist was Benjamin Senior Godines, who was a member of the Portuguese community of Amsterdam; some of his other works are also known.

The three pictures were conceived in the vein of the popular contemporary artistic genre of *vanitas* or *memento mori* (in Latin, 'remember that you will die'), which has been carefully 'Judaised' but still retains some Christian overtones. The first picture (JM 895.1) depicts an elegantly dressed young Sephardi Jew, attended by his black servant, juxtaposed with a decaying corpse, above which hover birds of prey. The straightforward moral is reinforced by the Hebrew verses written in the background, a reminder that the good life is a fast-fleeing illusion, and that God's judgment is stern. In addition to the ample use of Hebrew, the background of the image is reminiscent of the famous cemetery of the community

in Oude Kirke (near Amsterdam) – the topic of a well-known *memento mori* painting by the noted Dutch artist Jacob van Ruisdael (c.1628–1682). The second picture (JM 895.2) revolves around a biblical figure – Isaac. The willingness of Isaac to be sacrificed is depicted on the right, and his 'reward' on the left – Isaac is sowing the field and reaping a hundredfold harvest. Inscribed with the telling words 'Blessed are you when you come in and blessed are you when you go out' (Deuteronomy 28:6), the central gateway serves as a symbol of transition from this world to the next and the reward of the just as they enter the world to come, or Paradise. The third and last image (JM 895.3) is divided into three sections, relating to the practice of charity and its rewards: giving alms (left); a palm tree – symbol of the prosperous righteous person (based on Psalms 92:13; centre); and the scales of justice (right), thus emphasising the common root of the Hebrew words for justice and charity. This series of pictures represents an attempt by the Amsterdam Sephardim of the late seventeenth century to make sense of the life cycle in a traditional Jewish way through the idiom of their own place and time.

*Right:*
**SCENES FROM THE LIFE OF ISAAC**
245 x 386 mm
In the centre, a gateway inscribed with a blessing. On the right Abraham is about to sacrifice Isaac, while on the left Isaac is sowing in the fields.
JM 895.2

*Right:*
**TRIPTYCH**
245 x 386 mm
Three scenes viewed through a colonnade: on the left, two hands give alms through a curtain (showing the virtue of charity performed in secret); in the centre, a palm tree bearing the Ten Commandments; on the right, the scales of justice.
JM 895.3

# THE ALFRED RUBENS COLLECTION

## OF PRINTS AND DRAWINGS

David Bindman

The collection bequeathed to the Jewish Museum by Alfred
Rubens (1903–1998) consists of about 1,600 works on paper –
drawings, engravings, etchings, lithographs – all representing
Jewish people or aspects of Jewish life. About half of the
collection is made up of portraits, providing the basis for Rubens's
*Anglo-Jewish Portraits* (1935), while the rest formed the material
for his *A Jewish Iconography* (1954); both works were
consolidated and enlarged into the 1981 edition of the latter.

The rich collection of prints depicting the variety of Jewish costume around the world also heavily informs Rubens's *A History of Jewish Costume* (1967). Rubens acquired and catalogued every image he could find pertaining to Jews in any age or country, scouring the print shops of London and elsewhere over a fifty-year period when there was an abundance of material available at modest prices. Most of the material is of documentary and historical interest – portraits of worthies, views of synagogues, costume plates and caricatures – but there are some striking rarities and a few distinguished works of art, which are the focus of this essay.

Inevitably there is a predominance of English prints, not only because most of the collection was bought in London but also because of the extraordinary number of prints produced in that city in the eighteenth and nineteenth centuries. The collection is exceptionally rich in images of the great Jewish boxers of the late eighteenth and early nineteenth centuries. Notable individuals such as Lord George Gordon, Daniel Mendoza, the Rothschilds and Benjamin Disraeli are represented in depth, but in my view the most thought-provoking part of the collection is the large group of visual satires and caricatures. All the great caricaturists are represented; there are several watercolours as well as prints by Thomas Rowlandson, and there are unrecorded prints by the great late eighteenth-century prodigy Richard Newton, who died at the age of twenty-one.

Todd Endelman, in the Norton Lecture delivered at the Jewish Museum in 2001, argued that before photography caricatures were virtually the only images that responded to the flow of contemporary events, moods and fashions. They were not 'truthful' in any real sense, for they relied on exaggeration and crude simplification and, in the case of Jews, traditional stereotypes. Yet it is also clear that the representation of Jews in English caricature cannot be reduced to simple 'Otherness' from the dominant population, standing for everything that is evil and undesirable. Jews were sometimes cast as criminals, deceivers and seducers of innocence, but they were also the object of comic ridicule similar to that experienced by virtually all foreign groups at one time or another. When Jews are represented as demonic, it is in response to particular historical circumstances, and to the development in the late eighteenth century of modern conceptions of race.

***NEUE SCHWARM GEISTER-BRUT* ('A NEW SWARM OF RIGHTEOUS SPAWN')**
Germany, mid-seventeenth century
Etching
190 x 152 mm
Attack on various 'Judaising' sects, also referring to the return of Jews to England following their readmission by Oliver Cromwell. Inscription reads: '1. The Quaker is prone, stretched out by his spirit. He trembles, he froths and quakes, his limbs rock. [Probably George Fox, founder of the Society of Friends] 2. The Ranter makes of himself a fool and a God. God is in every tree. His crazy platoon rushes past. [Perhaps Thomas Tany, who believed in the restoration of the Jews to Jerusalem] 3. The Robins wants to elevate himself above God the Father and states that his pregnant wife will deliver the Messiah. [John Robins had himself proclaimed King of Israel and believed he had been chosen to lead the Jews back to Israel] 4. The Jew is also there, with his money-bags, and inquires the price of St Paul's Church.'
AR 810

# DUKE'S PLACE AND THE CITY FINANCIERS

The heart of the Jewish community in the early eighteenth century was to be found in the area around Duke's Place in the City of London, where the families involved in city finance lived. They formed an industrious and respectable community, but Jewish merchants had long been the subject of satire. In a German print (AR 810) contemporary with Cromwell's readmission of the Jews, a figure in the background represents the scurrilous belief of the time that they had put in an offer to buy St Paul's Cathedral: 'The Jew finds himself with his gold, and asks how much would Paul's Church cost?' (*Das Judlein findt sich auch mit seienem geld herbeij, und fragt, wir theuer doch die PAULUS Kirche seij*).

Despite the role that the City community played in arranging finance for controversial government ventures, it managed to keep itself fairly well out of the public eye in the first half of the

eighteenth century. A unique insight into its dynamics is given by the elaborate satirical print *The Jerusalem Infirmary – Alias a Journey to the Valley of Jehosophat* of 1749 (AR 819), which attacks the management of the hospital for the community's poor. Some individuals are identifiable, but inevitably many of the references are lost. The engraver of the print was presumably one of the many political satirists of the time, working from detailed instructions by someone party to the scandal. The Jews' Naturalisation Bill of 1753, known as 'The Jew Bill', which sought to allow foreign Jews to apply for British citizenship, brought the community under public scrutiny and produced dozens of hostile pamphlets and a great many satires, of which more than twelve are in the Rubens collection. Predictably, they are full of references to avarice, circumcision, pigs and the return to Jerusalem, and many of them saw in

the bill the hand of the most famous government loan contractor of the day, Samson Gideon (1699–1762). The most elaborate of these prints, *A Prospect of the New Jerusalem* (AR 821), has St Paul's dominating the City of London as a gleaming prospect in the distance. The Jews are identified by pointy beards, and are lightly caricatured, as in most other 'Jew Bill' prints, but otherwise they are shown as little different from non-Jews.

*Opposite:*
**THE JERUSALEM INFIRMARY –
ALIAS A JOURNEY TO THE VALLEY
OF JEHOSOPHAT**
England, 1749
Possibly commissioned by
Dr Meyer Löw Schomber
Engraving
383 x 225 mm
Satirical attack on the management of the Beth Holim, the hospital for the poor. It was published shortly after the hospital opened, and was accompanied by a sixteen-page 'play' full of scurrilous gossip. Below the print there is a key to the identities of numbered figures, which forms a puzzle to be solved by reference to the play.
AR 819

*Right:*
**A PROSPECT OF THE NEW JERUSALEM**
England, 1753
Engraving
311 x 234 mm
A group of Jews (and others?) looking towards London, with St Paul's Cathedral prominent on the horizon. In the foreground sits a Devil holding a sack labelled '£50,000'.
AR 821

A PROSPECT OF THE NEW JERUSALEM

Why, Friend, 'tis here in Print, the year too, See,
One Thousand Seven hundred Fifty Three,
Christ Save us from his Enemies the Jews!
What's this made free and true born English Jews!

The Devil, Infidels, Hereticks, and Turks!
These can't be English, these are Romish works:
Some Popish Plot to bring in the Pretender;
Pray Heaven guard our glorious Faith's Defender!

Numb. Chap. XXXII . Let this land be given unto thy Servants, for a Possession:

Price 6

# THE PEDLAR AND THE OLD CLOTHES MAN

From the 1750s the Jewish pedlar became a symbol of widespread unease concerning the impact of commercial culture on traditional values, but his itinerant life evoked also the legend of the Wandering Jew, condemned to wander throughout the world because of his failure to show compassion to Jesus carrying the Cross. In caricatures the pedlar wears a broad-brimmed hat and pointy beard, and he is the butt of endless puerile jokes about his horror of (or sometimes secret longing for) pigs and pork, and denial of and hatred for Christianity. He is ever in pursuit of 'monish' or money, preying on dissolute gentry and paupers alike. He is as much out of place in the countryside as a London alderman in a country cottage and therefore the butt of rustic humour, as in Richard Newton's *Tricks upon Travellers* of 1795 (AR 1083), where simple-minded villagers have put a piglet into a pedlar's box to attract the unwelcome attentions of a sow. On the other hand, until late in the century Jews were generally pictured with no more ridicule or hostility than the French, Italians, Irish and Scots, all of whom were reduced to comic stereotypes.

Jewish pedlars were part of the spectrum of urban life, like black domestic servants and elegantly dressed and bewigged Frenchmen.

Such prints are more silly than sinister, but there is an edgier note in many early nineteenth-century caricatures that goes beyond comic derision towards the suggestion that Jews are a relentlessly destructive force working their way into society. Sexual defilement, lechery and greed are, for instance, combined in Rowlandson's *Introduction or Moses with a Good Bargain,* of 1806 (AR 919), where an apparently innocent girl is being offered by either her mother or a bawd to an ungainly and lecherous Jew dressed in fashionable City attire. The upwardly mobile and sinister Jew bulging out of ill-fitting but ostentatious clothing reaches an apotheosis in a powerful Rowlandson watercolour of around 1810 (AR 930), inscribed 'Jew Merchants', in which three figures in a grand interior represent the transition from foreign pedlar (the fur-clad elderly figure on the right) to the fat and prosperous would-be gentleman (in the middle), accompanied by his coarse wife,

yawning loudly. The transition from rags to riches is underlined by an elaborately framed portrait group behind them, representing three pedlars with sacks and money bags, perhaps a reminder of their former way of life. Such images have a demonic force that takes them beyond humour, and this is palpable in the deeply sinister figure, also by Rowlandson, of *A Jew Broker* of 1801 (AR 906), with his malevolently staring eyes, standing in Duke's Place.

*Above left:*
**JEW MERCHANTS**
Thomas Rowlandson, England,
*c.*1810
Watercolour
277 x 219 mm
Drawing of three merchants, inscribed with the title in ink, and signed by Rowlandson.
AR 930

*Above right:*
**A JEW BROKER**
Thomas Rowlandson, England,
1 January 1801
Etching
317 x 222 mm
Caricature of a broker in the City of London.
AR 906

RAISING THE WIND.

" "When Noblemen have lost Race horse, and all their Rino spent,
Then little Isaac draws the Bond, and lends for Cent per Cent."

These images may represent a hysterical response to the growing assimilation of Jews into the professions, but they also invoke an irreducible physiological difference; the Jew is seen not as a figure of fun but as a physical antitype with alien values. In a print by Rowlandson, *Raising the Wind*, of 1812 (AR 939), a rosy-cheeked young gentleman offers the title deeds of his palatial house to two grotesquely caricatured Jewish moneylenders. A contrast is established between the young man's regular features, glowing pink skin and open countenance and the Jews' bearded features, sallow skin and shifty demeanour, though they wear respectable wigs and clothing. This contrast of a 'Christian' physical type with a 'degenerate' Jewish type can be seen in a caricature by a young German artist who worked in London in that decade, J. H. Ramberg (1763–1840), who was heavily influenced by Rowlandson and Gillray. *The Triumph,* of 1788 (AR 1833), is a satire on the boxing match that had taken place a few days earlier between the great Jewish boxer Daniel Mendoza and his rival Richard Humphries. Most prints of Mendoza were, as we will see, not unsympathetic to him, but this one celebrates

The TRIUMPH

*Top left:*
**RAISING THE WIND**
Thomas Rowlandson, England,
1812
Etching
299 x 228 mm
Two caricatured Jews arranging
a loan with a fashionable young
man.
AR 939

*Left:*
**THE TRIUMPH**
J. H. Ramberg, England,
7 January 1788
Etching
321 x 467 mm
Satire on the first boxing match
between Daniel Mendoza and
Richard Humphries.
AR 1833

*Above:*

**A GOOD TIME-KEEPER**
William Heath, England,
29 May 1823
Etching
114 x 149 mm
A sailor bargaining with an old
clothes man over a watch.
AR 1152

*Below right:*

**THE MAN WOT KNOWS HOW
TO DRIVE A BARGAIN**
'A. Sharpshooter', London,
14 July 1829
Etching
332 x 222 mm
Caricature representing Nathan
Mayer Rothschild as a dealer in
old clothes.
AR 2142

racial types, but it could be applied only too easily to them, and caricaturists such as Ramberg and Rowlandson seized upon these implications immediately.

This is not to say that such 'racial' caricature drove out that of the pedlar, who continued to appear in satire and pictures of street life well into the nineteenth century. The pedlar with a box of goods metamorphosed into the old clothes man, distinguished by his wearing on his head several hats piled on top of each other. He often appears in the many publications on street criers and salesmen of London, and in caricatures, as in William Heath's *A Good Time-Keeper*, of 1823 (AR 1152), where a man with the characteristic three hats bargains with a sailor over a watch. Such an image proved irresistible to the caricaturist 'A. Sharpshooter' in 1829 (AR 2142) when faced with the famous banker Nathan Mayer Rothschild, who is shown, his face only slightly caricatured, in the guise of a pedlar, with a sack marked 'French Rentes £20,000', wearing two hats, one of which is inscribed 'Policy & Assurance'.

'Humphries the Victorious who in a bloody fight overcame the 12 tribes of Israel'. Humphries, carried aloft by his supporters, exhibits an ideal grace and physiognomy, while the defeated Mendoza is given a pointed beard that emphasises his resemblance to the Jewish supporter who laments over him. The prominent convert Lord George Gordon, his straight 'English' profile emphasised, is absorbed in a copy of the Talmud.

Why does this sharp physiognomical difference emerge in the 1780s? One reason could be the development of racial theories on the Continent, but more immediately it was probably due to the enormous impact of the publication, first in Switzerland and then in Britain and France, of the Swiss theologian Johann Caspar Lavater's book *An Essay on Physiognomy*, first published in English in 1789, translated from a German edition of the previous decade. While it had long been commonplace to suggest that a person's character could be read from his or her appearance, Lavater argued that it could be scientifically demonstrated that facial features were an index to the soul or to a person's moral being; the more beautiful the face, the more beautiful the soul, and conversely an ugly face was a clear sign of a bad moral character. Lavater's theory was not explicitly directed toward ethnic or

A SCIENTIFIC ACCOUNT of the concluding BATTLE between those Champions of the Fist, DANIEL MENDOZA and RICHARD HUMPHREYS, fought at DONCASTER, on Wednesday, the 29th of September, 1790.

*THE MENDOZA–HUMPHRIES FIGHT OF 29 SEPTEMBER 1790*
James Gillray, England, 9 October 1790
Etching  228 x 349 mm

Scene of a boxing match between Daniel Mendoza and Richard Humphries, with the names of the chief figures given below. A printed account of the fight is attached.
AR 1846

# Jewish Celebrities and Crypto-Jews

A number of well-known musicians such as the cellist Giacobbe Cervetto (d.1783; always called 'Nosey') and the singer John Braham (1774–1856) were known to be Jewish, and many portraits of them can be found in the Rubens collection. However, the greatest Jewish celebrity of the eighteenth century was the boxer Daniel Mendoza (1763–1836), whose fame inspired a number of other Jewish boxers, such as Samuel Elias (1775–1816), known as 'Dutch Sam', and his son of the same name, who fought as 'Young Dutch Sam'. The thirty-nine images of Mendoza in the Rubens collection attest to the boxer's fame. These visual records and caricatures were centred around his three epic bouts with his chief opponent, Richard Humphries, with the first, on 9 January 1788, decided in favour of Humphries, while the second, on 6 May 1789,

and the final one, on 29 September 1790, were both won by Mendoza. In contrast to the hostility of Ramberg's satire on the first contest, those by other artists and satirists were by and large sympathetic to Mendoza, despite the sometimes double-edged references to his 'superior skill' rather than brute strength. In Gillray's version of the 29 September 1790 fight, published on 9 October 1790 (AR 1846), praise was given for 'The Manner in Which Mendoza Caught Humphries twice & Generously laid him down without taking the advantage of his Situation'. The most powerful representation is Gillray's heroic portrait of him alone in the ring, his fists raised (AR 1851), one of the rare occasions on which the artist did not resort to satire; nor did he emphasise the 'Jewishness' of Mendoza's physiognomy.

**MENDOZA**
James Gillray, London, late eighteenth century
Aquatint
95 x 70 mm
Full-length portrait of Daniel Mendoza in the ring, in a fighting attitude; spectators behind.
AR 1851

The only Jewish people who rivalled Mendoza in celebrity in eighteenth- and early nineteenth-century Britain were Christians who had converted to Judaism. The reasons that a number did so derived from the millenarian Protestant belief in the literal truth of the biblical Book of Revelation, and that the Messiah will only return when the Jews are scattered across the whole world and are in the Last Days converted to Christianity. In troubled times, such as the period of the Civil War and Protectorate in the seventeenth century, and the French Revolution in the 1790s, small numbers of fanatical Protestants either converted to Judaism or sought to lead the Jews back to Jerusalem, there to rebuild the Holy City and await the Resurrection. The most notorious of these converts was Lord George Gordon (1751–1793), son of the 3rd Duke of Gordon and a Member of Parliament, known for his fervent anti-Catholicism and leadership of the destructive Gordon Riots in 1780. Following some years on the run, he surfaced in Birmingham fully converted to Judaism; after a trial he spent his remaining years in Newgate Prison, where he became one of the sights of London and the subject of notable caricatures.

The Rubens collection contains the only recorded impression of the most magnificent of these, Richard Newton's *Soulagement en Prison, or, Comfort in Prison*, of 1793 (AR 1517), derived from the original watercolour now in the Lewis Walpole Library, Farmington, Connecticut. It shows Lord George presiding over a highly convivial gathering of radical writers and publishers, all of whom are identified. As a prisoner on the 'state side' of Newgate from a wealthy family, Lord George was able to receive visitors and entertain them to a strictly *kosher* table, occasionally employing a Scottish piper. The appealing scene in Newgate may be contrasted with Ramberg's version of Lord George's imprisonment, known from a later impression of the print in the Jewish Theological Seminary in New York, entitled *Moses Chusing his Cook*, which shows him as a fastidious gentleman tasting food proffered by sinister and grotesquely caricatured Jewish types.

**MOSES CHUSING HIS COOK**
J. H. Ramberg, London,
1 April 1803
Courtesy of The Library of The
Jewish Theological Seminary,
New York

**SOULAGEMENT EN PRISON,**
**OR, COMFORT IN PRISON**

Richard Newton, London,
20 August 1793
Aquatint
413 x 596 mm

Caricature showing Lord George
Gordon entertaining guests
in his room at Newgate Prison.
Each figure bears a number,
referring to a key below the
design. Lord George Gordon,
numbered 1, is seated at the
head of the table, smoking a
long clay pipe, wearing a large
hat and with a long beard.

AR 1517

The PROPHET of the HEBREWS, — the PRINCE of PEACE, conducting the JEWS to the PROMIS'D-LAND.

Gordon's fame was rivalled by that of the naval officer Richard Brothers, who, after an encounter with Satan on London's Tottenham Court Road and a heavenly vision, proclaimed himself 'Prince of the Hebrews and Nephew of the Almighty'. He worked actively to lead the Jews of Britain to Jerusalem on the understanding that the French Revolution was the opening phase of the apocalyptic destruction of the world, to be followed by the Last Judgement, as prophesied in the Book of Revelation. Such beliefs had a particular resonance for London craftsmen, and one follower, the engraver William Sharp, went to the trouble of having a special suit made with large pockets to carry his luggage on the way to Jerusalem. Gillray's caricature *The Prophet of the Hebrews – the Prince of Peace – Conducting the Jews to the Promis'd Land,* of 1795 (AR 206), shows Brothers as a demented fool carrying a flaming sword, a copy of Revelation and, in a sack

marked 'Bundle of the elect', Whig politicians on his back, while he tramples underfoot the Great Beast of Revelation. He leads a group of Jewish pedlars toward the gate of Jerusalem, which we can see as a gallows, while London is in flames behind him.

In the later nineteenth century Benjamin Disraeli was the most famous Jewish Briton; although he was brought up as a Christian, virtually all representations of him emphasise the Jewishness of his appearance, and occasionally references are made to traditional stereotypes. There is a hint of the rich pedlar in ill-fitting clothes in the 'Ape' (Carlo Pellegrini) cartoon in *Vanity Fair* of 30 January 1869 (C 1986.5.11), but it is by now only a distant echo. Although he was frequently caricatured, Disraeli was fortunate to seek power at a time when the brutal satire characteristic of the Hanoverian age was increasingly regarded as tasteless and ill-mannered.

Pre-Victorian English satires of Jews are not for the faint-hearted. They tend to be crude in their humour, demeaning to those who differ from the norm, and they occasionally become something more sinister in the late eighteenth and early nineteenth centuries, when ideas of race were developing across Europe. It is ironic that racial satire began to diminish just as ideas of racial character were achieving scientific plausibility, but this was because satire and not racism went out of fashion. Even so, as Endelman has noted, there is some comfort in the variety and unpredictability of English satire, and its ability to discriminate equally against all forms of difference, whatever their origin.

*Opposite:*
**THE PROPHET OF THE HEBREWS –
THE PRINCE OF PEACE –
CONDUCTING THE JEWS TO THE
PROMIS'D LAND**
James Gillray, London,
5 March 1795
Etching
237 x 346 mm
Caricature of Richard Brothers, published on the day following his arrest for treason on the grounds that he prophesied the death of the King. In the 'Bundle of the Elect' strapped on his back are the leaders of the Parliamentary Opposition: Stanhope and Lansdowne in the House of Lords, Fox and Sheridan in the House of Commons.
AR 206

*Right:*
**BENJAMIN DISRAELI**
Carlo Pellegrini ('Ape'), London,
30 January 1869
Chromolithograph
310 x 182 mm
*Vanity Fair* caricature of Disraeli, first in the 'Statesmen' series. Captioned: 'He educated the Tories and dished the Whigs to pass Reform, but to have become what he has is the greatest Reform of all.'
C 1986.5.11

VANITY FAIR.  Jan. 30, 1869.

No 13.  STATESMEN, No. 1.

" He educated the Tories and dished the Whigs to pass Reform, but to have
become what he is from what he was is the greatest Reform of all."

# MANUSCRIPT TREASURES

Ilana Tahan

The Jewish Museum counts among its treasures Hebrew manuscripts, many of which are embellished with illustrations, engravings or colourful miniatures. In this group belong *Purim* scrolls (*Megillot*), Passover liturgies (*Haggadot*), prayer books for various occasions and *Omer* calendars. With few exceptions, these decorated hand-made books were created in Europe. A major study of this specific group of manuscripts has yet to be undertaken.

This chapter will focus on a cluster of decorated items dating mostly from the seventeenth and eighteenth centuries, the latter period being regarded as the 'Renaissance' of Hebrew manuscript art. In order to understand the factors that affected the iconography and structure peculiar to these manuscripts, it is important to consider briefly the evolution of the Hebrew book from the arrival of printing in the mid-fifteenth century, up to and including the eighteenth century.

# HEBREW BOOK PRODUCTION, 1400–1800

After the invention of printing the production of hand-written books began to slow down considerably. Nevertheless, Hebrew manuscripts continued to be produced well into the last quarter of the fifteenth century, even though by then the printed book was already widely circulated. The exquisite Hebrew Bibles and legal codices illuminated at Lisbon in the 1470s and 1480s are a case in point.

Jews kept alive the tradition of manuscript production and the art of illumination in the centuries that followed, producing the texts required for religious practice and also two main types of manuscripts: illuminated marriage contracts, especially popular in Italy in the seventeenth and eighteenth centuries, and decorated *Purim* scrolls greatly sought after in Italy, Germany, the Netherlands and Central Europe from the late sixteenth century onwards.

Concurrently, during the sixteenth century demand for Hebrew printed books soared beyond expectation. The status of the book had been rapidly changing from a private commodity owned by few to a public, standardised domain.

In the early period of printing, illustration in Hebrew books was essentially modelled on the iconography and layouts of illuminated medieval manuscripts. The earliest illustrated printed books borrowed a variety of pictorial elements from their predecessors. The commonest were historiated letters (that is, letters adorned with the figures of humans, animals or birds, often for narrative purposes), ornamental headings and opulent decorative borders which were completed in type. Increasingly, sixteenth- and seventeenth-century books were adorned with monumental title pages and woodcut drawings occasionally coloured by hand. Fable books such as *Meshal ha-Kadmoni*, the book of religious customs for the Jewish year (*Sefer Minhagim*) and the Passover *Haggadah* in particular, became favourite vehicles for book illustration. Landmark editions such as the splendid Prague *Haggadah* issued in 1526 and the magnificent 1609 Venice *Haggadah*, replete with highly innovative woodcut illustrations, exerted an influence that would be felt for centuries to come.

**KETUBAH**
Venice, 1733
Parchment
546 x 432 mm
Marriage contract with a painted floral border, recording the marriage of Joseph, son of the late Moses Cohen del Medigo, to Rica, daughter of Isaac Pacifico.
JM 472

Throughout the first half of the sixteenth century Italy held centre stage in the diffusion of Hebrew books, and Venice became the most important centre of Hebrew printing. The seventeenth century witnessed the gradual rise of the Netherlands as the new custodians of the Jewish book, with Amsterdam as the predominant centre. According to Emile Schrijver, books printed in Amsterdam 'excelled above the standards reached by books printed elsewhere, especially from the aesthetic point of view'. The typographic and graphic techniques used in producing these books were innovative, sophisticated and attuned to contemporary taste. Amsterdam imprints, especially those coming off the presses of Solomon Proops and Joseph Athias, were often adorned with elaborate copper engravings surpassing in beauty the cruder, linear woodcuts employed elsewhere.

The 1695 edition of the *Haggadah* illustrated by Abraham bar Yaakov, reprinted in 1712 with slight modifications, was virtually the first ever Passover *Haggadah* to contain copperplate engravings. The style and iconography of Amsterdam *Haggadot* served as perpetual models for later printed *Haggadot*, not least for the self-taught scribe–artists who emerged in the eighteenth century.

Amsterdam Hebrew types too achieved fame, to the extent that printers in other European lands repeatedly imitated them, proudly advertising on their books' title pages *Be-otiyot Amsterdam* ('with Amsterdam letters'), while hiding in small print the original place of printing – a cunning device intended to attract buyers and bolster sales of their books. In their turn eighteenth-century scribe–artists utilised the Amsterdam letters to write their manuscripts, and likewise displayed the flattering *Be-otiyot Amsterdam* 'logo' on their adorned frontispieces. This demonstrates the tremendous and lasting impact the Amsterdam Hebrew typography had on the development of the Hebrew book.

The flourishing of Hebrew manuscript art in the eighteenth century began in Austria, Bohemia and Moravia, and gradually spread westward, reaching Germany, the Netherlands and other areas. Ernest Namény maintains that this 'Renaissance' was a phenomenon unique in the history of art and singular to Judaism. He further claims that whereas the medieval illuminated manuscript was an object meant for study, the eighteenth-century painted book was an object of worship. Other scholars have linked the revival of Hebrew manuscript decoration to the emergence of a wealthy class of Central European 'Court Jews', who performed important functions for their gentile rulers and at the same time acted as representatives of their own communities.

Influenced by the culture and fashion prevailing in their Christian environment, well-to-do Jews began to commission painted manuscripts of texts required for everyday use, special occasions and life cycle events, leading apparently to the formation of a school of professional copyists–miniaturists. Commissions included *Haggadot*, prayers for various occasions, Grace after Meals blessings, community records, circumcisers' manuals, *Omer* calendars, scrolls of Esther and others. Their imagery was drawn from printed books (particularly the 1695 and 1712 Amsterdam *Haggadot*), which they re-interpreted and presented in a fresh, individualistic style based on contemporary trends. It is estimated that between 1720 and 1760 hundreds of illuminated handwritten books were produced, of which about 450 have survived. Notable copyists-illustrators who made a remarkable contribution to the revival of eighteenth–century manuscript art include Aryeh ben Judah Leib of Trebitsch, Moses Loeb ben Wolf of Trebitsch, Aaron ben Benjamin Herlingen of Gewitsch, Joseph ben David Leipnik, Jacob Sopher of Berlin and Samuel Dresnitz, to name just a few. Works by some of these artists have been preserved in the Jewish Museum's collection and are discussed below.

# PRAYER BOOKS

*Seder Keri'at Shema' 'al ha-mitah* ('Reading of the *Shema* and Prayers Recited before Retiring to Bed'; JM 631) is an eighteenth-century manuscript boasting a handsomely decorated title page, fine pen-and-ink illustrations, golden letters and elaborate initial words. On the frontispiece the letters of the word *Seder* are inscribed in three separate compartments, each with a different drawing as background. These are: a turreted contemporary fortress, a winged, semi-naked cherub holding the edge of the letter *dalet*, and a rich flower arrangement.

The angelic motif is duplicated on folio 10*v*, where an elegantly dressed guardian angel, a palm leaf in his left hand, is pictured against a walled city.

Though unsigned, the manuscript has been attributed to Samuel ben Zvi Hirsch Dresnitz, an important and prolific scribe–artist from Strassnitz in Moravia, who apparently began his artistic career in Vienna in or before 1724. Dresnitz produced a total of sixteen manuscripts, fifteen of which he completed between 1726 and 1755 while working as a ritual butcher in Nikolsburg.

*Below:*
**PRAYER BOOK** (frontispiece)
Samuel Dresnitz, Austria
or Moravia, early to
mid-eighteenth century
Paper, velvet
80 x 105 mm
JM 631

*Below:*
**PRAYER BOOK** (fol.10*v*)
Samuel Dresnitz, Austria
or Moravia, early to
mid-eighteenth century
Paper, velvet
80 x 105 mm
JM 631

**PRAYER BOOK** (fol.7v)
Samuel Dresnitz, Austria
or Moravia, early to
mid-eighteenth century
Paper, velvet
80 x 105 mm
JM 631

Dresnitz's craftsmanship is reflected not only in the carefully planned layout of pages, but also in the calligraphy of the text. Notable examples of his scribal skills are the ligatures used in writing the divine name, which appear as either a combination of the letters *aleph* and *lamed*, or as two letters *yod* with a ligature of *aleph/lamed* following it (for example fols. 4v–5r). The undulating, ripple-like lettering of the word *Va-yehi* (fol. 7v) provides additional proof of Dresnitz's masterly hand.

Comparison with other known works executed by this scribe–artist reveals certain characteristic traits. His initial letters inhabited by drawings of flora, fauna and buildings are evidently the most typical, and may have been inspired by historiated letters and architectural designs found in the Prague 1526 and Venice 1609 *Haggadot*. Dresnitz's works contain a variety of animals and birds, a common feature in other contemporary hand-painted books. Apart from rampant lions (as seen on fol.1v) and eagles with outstretched wings, he painted profiles of elephants and especially the crouching rabbits that seem to be his 'trademark'.

In terms of provenance, several inscriptions indicate that this manuscript was owned by at least three generations of the same family. The earliest known owner was Gella, wife of Raphael Segal Sinzheim of Vienna, who was related to the wife of David Tevele Schiff, the Chief Rabbi of the Great Synagogue, London, between 1765 and 1792. Raphael Sinzheim appears to have died in 1752, which suggests that our manuscript pre-dates that year.

*Seder Birkat ha-mazon 'im tikun keri'at Shema* ('Grace after Meals and Other Daily Prayers', with rubrics in Yiddish; JM 630) is a pleasing manuscript executed in the Bohemian/Moravian style of the eighteenth century. The monumental frontispiece was modelled on the engraved title pages of the Amsterdam 1695 and 1712 *Haggadot*. Aaron and Moses flank the portal of the title, which is surmounted by a cartouche guarded by two vultures. The cartouche was probably left blank for the name of a potential buyer. In the lower section two panels contain what appear to be Bohemian or Moravian townscapes, reminiscent of those found in the 1526 Prague *Haggadah*. There are several fine textual illustrations executed in pen and ink, as for instance the candelabrum next to the '*Al ha-Nisim* Prayer Recited at *Hanukah* (fol. 3v), and the woman reading her prayers by candle light before retiring to bed (fol. 24v). The text is copied in minute script in greyish ink. This manuscript was completed in Mannheim in 1745 by Simha Pöhm, or Simha of Bohemia, a minor yet talented calligrapher–miniaturist who was responsible for at least two other extant manuscripts.

A miniature book of benedictions for daily use (JM 630a) is among the most memorable manuscripts in the Museum collection and a very good example of an eighteenth-century commissioned piece copied 'with Amsterdam letters'. The manuscript was evidently intended as a wedding gift from the groom, Zachariah Fränkel of Fürth, to his bride, Frumet Kahn of Frankfurt, and is dated 1734. The anonymous scribe–artist has immortalised the couple and their union on the first title page

*Left:*
**PRAYER BOOK**
(first title page)
Frankfurt, 1734
Parchment, leather
97 x 74 mm
JM 630a

of the manuscript. There is a second title page based on the traditional Amsterdam models showing nonetheless a slight iconographic modification. Moses appears here bare-headed, with horns beaming out of his hair. A third frontispiece titled *Tikun keri'at Shema' 'al ha-mitah* ('Prayers before Retiring to Bed', fol.14r) features Kings David and Solomon crowned and dressed in regal finery, and in the lower margin the mark of excellence – *Be-otiyot Amsterdam*. The miniatures were probably painted by two artists whose styles and skills differ greatly. The first artist is likely to have been responsible for the somewhat naive yet expressive scenes in the manuscript, one such example being the group of drinkers on folio 9v. The second, more accomplished artist painted elegantly creating charming, graceful figures and delicate décors. The two men carrying a large vine (fol.10v), and the maiden with two ewers

*Above:*
**PRAYER BOOK** (fol.14r)
Frankfurt, 1734
Parchment, leather
97 x 74 mm
JM 630a

*Above:*
**PRAYER BOOK** (fol. 9*v*)
Frankfurt, 1734
Parchment, leather
97 x 74 mm
JM 630a

*Above:*
**PRAYER BOOK** (fol. 10*v*)
Frankfurt, 1734
Parchment, leather
97 x 74 mm
JM 630a

(fol. 20*v*) are very fine examples of his artistry. According to the owners' inscriptions, the manuscript changed hands at least four times. Its most recent owner was Arthur Ellis Franklin (1857–1938), a banker and prominent Anglo-Jewish communal worker, whose important ritual art collection was acquired by The Jewish Museum, London, in 1967.

One of the gems in the collection and a superb example of commissioned art is undoubtedly the *Grace after Meals, Blessings and Keri'at Shema'* (C 1985.7.1) copied and illuminated in Vienna in 1742 by Aaron Wolf Herlingen of Gewitsch. He lived in Pressburg and Vienna, where for nearly twenty-eight years (1724–52) he created several dozen enchanting manuscripts, many of which have survived. For several years he was employed by the Imperial Library of Vienna copying and decorating some significant Hebrew and non-Hebrew manuscripts. Herlingen is regarded as the most prolific scribe–artist of the eighteenth-century Moravian school, and its most talented calligrapher and penman. Some of his

best pieces were executed in sepia, but he is also known to have produced colourful manuscripts. His art is a fusion of traditional themes reworked in contemporary Rococo fashion.

This richly decorated manuscript was ordered by a Sephardi nobleman, Moses Lopes Pereyra, 2nd Baron d'Aguilar, to commemorate the circumcision of his son Ephraim Hayim. The handsome frontispiece features the usual portraits of Moses and Aaron flanking the title panel, and two medallions positioned in the upper and lower sections. The lower medallion contains an inscription naming Ephraim Hayim as the owner. According to Vivian Mann of The Jewish Museum, New York, the upper, blank medallion was intended for a guest's name, thus implying that this type of manuscript would have served as 'books of blessings do today – as remembrances of life cycle occasions'. A detailed colophon provides information about the place and date of the event (Vienna, 5 *Elul* 1737, Spoyns Haus, in Alten Flies Markt Street), and some of those present at that special celebration. Two exquisite gold leaf

*Above:*
**PRAYER BOOK** (frontispiece)
Aaron Wolf Herlingen, Vienna, 1742
Parchment, leather
110 x 75 mm
C 1985.7.1

cartouches executed in Rococo style can be found on folios *2r* and *8r*. The former encloses the blessing *Barukh hu u-barukh shemo u-barukh zikhro* and is embellished with grape clusters. The latter encapsulates the title *Seder Keri'at Shema' shel laylah* and is enhanced with vibrant blue and golden flowers. The impeccable Hebrew lettering of the vocalised text is the work of a master calligrapher. The beautifully tooled gilded binding adds a touch of luxury to the manuscript. The whole piece is imbued with elegance and opulence, indicating that no expense was spared here.

*Above right:*
**PRAYER BOOK** (fol. *2r*)
Aaron Wolf Herlingen, Vienna, 1742
Parchment, leather
110 x 75 mm
C 1985.7.1

*Right:*
**PRAYER BOOK** (fol. *8r*)
Aaron Wolf Herlingen, Vienna, 1742
Parchment, leather
110 x 75 mm
C 1985.7.1

# PASSOVER *HAGGADOT*

Since medieval times the *Haggadah* has been a rich source of inspiration for artistic creativity, and it remains one of the most frequently illustrated texts in the Jewish liturgy.

The Jewish Museum holds a small number of *Haggadah* manuscripts, two of which are discussed here. The first, JM 632, was copied and illustrated in 1769 by the most famous Hungarian proponent of eighteenth-century Hebrew manuscript art, Hayim ben Asher Anshel of Kittsee. Hayim Anshel began his career as a teacher, and later became a congregational clerk. Between 1741 and 1782 he worked mainly as a scribe–artist in Kittsee and in Pressburg. Twenty-seven of his works are known to have survived in collections around the world. The example in the Jewish Museum lacks textual illustrations, which is a distinctive trait of *Haggadot* by this artist. Its twenty-three miniatures are essentially variations on a dominant motif that defines Hayim Anshel's art, namely colourful floral ornamentations combining Rococo and local popular elements. Ernest Namény maintains that 'The flora of all the countries of Europe where Jews lived is represented here.'

The finely wrought frontispiece is modelled on the Amsterdam prototypes but features additional elements also found in Anshel's other work. These include Rococo medallions surmounted by shells and flanked by winged eagles and architectural niches sheltering Moses and Aaron. There is a sense of symmetry and charm emanating from the pages of this *Haggadah*, which may be partially due to the neat calligraphy and the confident way in which the scribe handles square and Rashi scripts.

The second *Haggadah*, JM 639a, was handwritten and illustrated in 1756 by Abraham Sopher of Ihringen, a calligrapher–miniaturist from Alsace. Its decorative programme differs somewhat from other eighteenth-century works discussed so far, as it is based almost entirely on the 1609 Venice *Haggadah*. Many of its pages display architectural portals, attractive text illustrations captioned in Yiddish rhymes and charming historiated initials, all modelled on the Venetian woodcuts. These are interspersed with contemporary folkloristic designs, particularly colourful floral and vegetal ornaments executed in watercolours in pastel shades. Abraham Sopher was evidently a skilled scribe–artist, and overall this is a very pleasing work.

*HAGGADAH*
Abraham Sopher, Germany,
1756
Parchment, leather
318 x 210 mm
JM 639a

היום תשעה עשר יום
לעומר:
שהם שני שבויות
וחמישה ימים:

היום עשרים יום לעומר
שהם שני שבויות
וששה ימים

יום אחד ועשרים יום
לעומר:
שהם שלשה שבועות:

## OMER CALENDARS

Decorated calendars are used for counting the *Omer*, the seven-week period between Passover and *Shavuot*. The Jewish Museum holds an eighteenth-century *Omer* calendar in scroll format (JM 364), which, in accordance with an old Sephardi tradition, would have previously been encased in a cabinet meant to hang on a wall. The parchment scroll features three horizontal rows of square compartments with captions written in Sephardi square script. The panels in the upper row enumerate the days of the *Omer* in sequence, while the middle and lower panels count respectively the weeks and days of the week. The compartments are embellished with simple illustrations of fruits and flowers executed in pastel colours. The dominant floral motifs are tulips, suggesting a Dutch provenance.

A rather unusual *Omer* book is the *Seder Sefirat ha-'Omer* (JM 633) completed between 1802 and 1804 by Yitshak son of Mehalalel. It contains the usual formula for counting the *Omer* each day and, on most of the opposite pages, biblical scenes bearing no relation whatsoever to the actual text. The forty-nine coloured miniatures are very crude and of no aesthetic merit. Additionally, there are several non-biblical, sepia illustrations that were probably cut out from contemporary books and pasted down in the manuscript (for example, one facing the title page and another on fol. 55*r*). The images, captioned in Italian, depict domestic scenes with fashionably dressed couples. The captions refer to women's attributes, which may suggest that the manuscript was meant for a lady. This rare specimen is an interesting example of early nineteenth-century Hebrew manuscript art and belongs to a group of six similar Italian *Omer* books held in various collections.

***OMER* SCROLL**
Netherlands, eighteenth century
Parchment
0.28 x 3.9 m
JM 364

# *PURIM* SCROLLS

The story of *Purim* is told in the Book of Esther, traditionally written in the form of scrolls known in Hebrew as *Megillot Esther*. The scrolls intended for synagogue reading are always unadorned, but personal *Purim* scrolls may be richly decorated. The earliest of this type were apparently produced in Italy in the second half of the sixteenth century, but only about four specimens from that period are known to have survived. None of these extremely rare *Megillot* contained characters or narrative scenes of the *Purim* story, but interestingly they were all decorated with copperplate engraved borders. The transition from *Purim* scroll decoration to *Purim* scroll illustration occurred only in the early seventeenth century.

The Museum's collection includes several beautifully engraved and illuminated Esther scrolls. Nowhere is the art of copperplate engraving better represented than in an Esther scroll designed by Salom Italia, or d'Italia (JM 282). The most famous Hebrew manuscript artist of the seventeenth century, Italia was born in 1619 in Mantua and was probably descended from a family of printers. In 1641 he settled in Amsterdam, where he began his engraving career, producing eighteen works in a span of fourteen years.

An elaborate and impressive piece, the Jewish Museum Esther scroll was probably engraved after 1647 and shows Italia's most typical and influential innovations. These consist of archways, probably modelled on triumphal monuments, full-length figures from the *Purim* narrative between the text panels, and the use of landscape and townscape vignettes in the borders. There is a fusion of Italianate and Dutch motifs in this scroll. The architectural portals were styled in the Italian fashion, topped by broken pediments supporting reclining female figures holding palm leaves. The Dutch elements, such as ships and windmills, can be seen in the lower vignettes. Italia's innovative approach exerted an enormous influence on the decoration of later European *Purim* scrolls, whether engraved or hand-painted.

An engraved specimen that may have been inspired by Salom Italia's art is a parchment Esther scroll that was hand-written in 1782 near Prague (JM 304). The text is separated by twisted Baroque columns surmounted by floral urns and characters from the Esther story. The upper and lower sections feature a repeating pattern of elaborate scroll medallions encapsulating Dutch landscapes, alternating with female nudes, birds and foliage. The opening section of the scroll comprises two engraved scenes from the story. This is an important example of a *Megillah* with copperplate engraved borders designed by an unknown artist, possibly of Dutch origin.

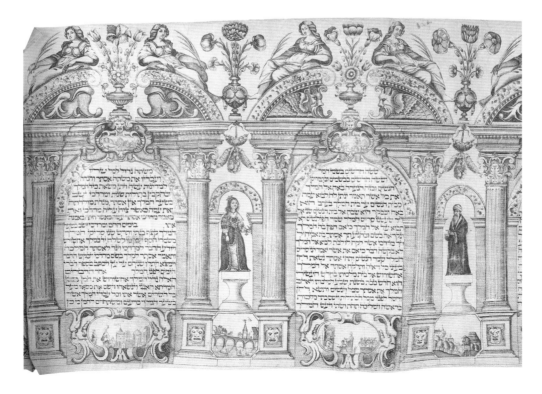

*MEGILLAH* (detail)
Salom Italia, Amsterdam,
mid-seventeenth century
Wood, parchment
*Megillah* scroll on a wooden roller
with baluster finials.
JM 282

Another of the greatest treasures in the Esther scrolls collection (JM 291) is a superb example of eighteenth-century Rococo art. The text of this lavishly illuminated scroll is written within arches, decorated with garlands and flanked by twisted columns. In the upper section allegorical female figures are seated on scrolled thrones above arches. The figures are interspersed with winged cherubs flanking cartouches topped by crowns, decorated with fruits and branches. In the lower section, below the text panels, are vignettes with scenes illustrating the dramatic events of the *Purim* narrative. The artist of this glorious, profusely decorated scroll is unknown; however, he may have been responsible for several other very similar pieces currently held in collections overseas. The style of the paintings, the details of dress and the ornamental motifs suggest a north Italian origin.

The Jewish Museum's manuscripts, and especially the prayer books, *Haggadot*, *Omer* calendars and *Megillot* described here, constitute a unique and significant resource. They demonstrate a wide range of trends in manuscript decoration over time and across the continent of Europe, allowing us to trace stylistic relationships within the Hebrew manuscript tradition and also with other types of books. They offer an insight into the lives of those who made and used them, and of course they are beautiful objects in their own right.

**MEGILLAH** (detail)
North Italy (?), eighteenth century
Ivory, parchment
Roller 648 mm long; scroll
0.42 x 4.37 m
*Megillah* scroll on an ivory roller carved with a decorated head and fluted handle.
JM 291

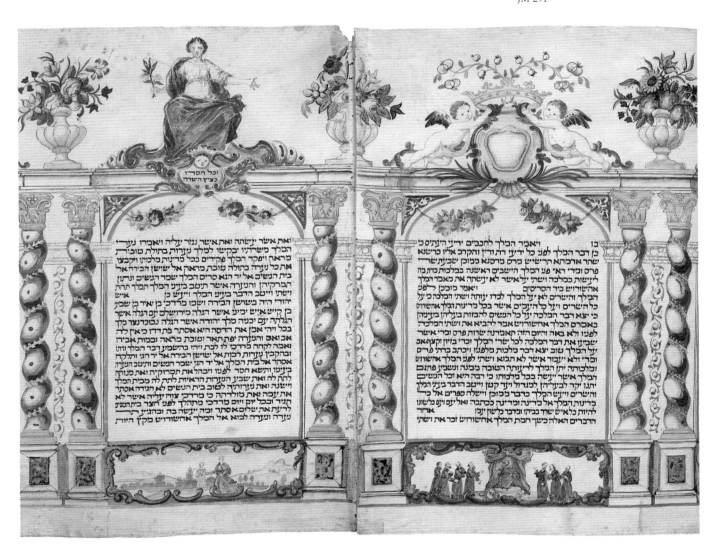

# THE JEWISH
# EAST END

Anne J. Kershen

Jewish settlement at the eastern edge of the City of London
began following the Readmission of Jews to England by Oliver
Cromwell in 1656. However, it was not until the closing
decades of the nineteenth century, when immigration from
Eastern Europe was at its height, that the area became known
as the 'Jewish East End' – and by some as 'Little Jerusalem'.
As far back as the seventeenth century immigrants to the
capital had traditionally settled in the district known as
Spitalfields, an area of some 200 acres that lay at the western
edge of what is today the London Borough of Tower Hamlets.
It was here that the Jewish community established its roots.

As the number of Eastern European immigrants increased in the years between 1881 and the outbreak of the First World War, the Jewish East End became readily identifiable. It is estimated that in 1880 there were about 46,000 Jews in London, but by 1900 this figure had almost trebled to 135,000, most of whom were housed within the two square miles of the East End. In 1889 Charles Booth recorded: 'The newcomers have gradually replaced the English population in whole districts, Hanbury Street, Fashion Street, Pelham Street, and many streets and lanes and alleys have fallen before them; they have introduced new trades as well as new habits and they live and crowd together.' In his book *Living London*, published in three volumes between 1901 and 1906, G. R. Sims commented: 'It is its utterly alien aspect that strikes you first and foremost. For the Ghetto is a fragment of Poland torn off from Central Europe and dropped haphazard into the heart of Britain.'

The influx of Jewish immigrants resulted from a combination of fear of persecution and economic hardship. From the 1830s most Russian Jews had to reside in the Pale of Settlement, an area of western Russia between the Baltic and the Black Sea. They were gradually forced out of their villages and into towns, where it became increasingly difficult to make a living. Following the assassination of Tsar Alexander II in 1881, they were subject to *pogroms*: violent mass attacks, often officially instigated. The worst attack occurred in Odessa in 1905, when 300 were killed and thousands wounded. Many immigrants also fled to avoid forcible conscription into the Russian army, where they faced twenty-five years' service in brutal conditions. At the same time they also sought to improve their economic situation and to make a new life.

*Opposite:*
**BAKING EQUIPMENT**
London, *c.*1935–85
Tin, wood, hessian
Tins 270 x 110 x 100 mm
These tools were used at Goldring's Bakery, which was established in the early 1920s by Polish-Jewish immigrant, Jacob Goldring, in Mile End, East London.
T 118

*Below:*
**GOULSTON STREET ON SUNDAY MORNING**
From *Living London*,
G. R. Sims, 1901
Photograph
A street market in Whitechapel at the height of the Great Migration.
1060.9

# RELIGION

There are two prerequisites for a Jewish community: a house of prayer and a consecrated burial ground. There had been synagogues on the boundaries of the City and Spitalfields since the seventeenth century. With their dog-collared reverends, emphasis on decorum, anglicised and socially elevated members and high membership fees, these synagogues were eschewed by the Eastern European immigrants, who saw them as tools of anglicisation rather than places of religious observance. The arrival of impoverished Jews from the Netherlands, Central and Eastern Europe resulted in the establishment of synagogues closer to the location and likings of the newer immigrants. Even before the mass influx of immigrants in the 1880s and 1890s there were a number of *hevrot* (small synagogues) in Spitalfields. These included Sandys Row (established in 1851), Princes (Princelet) Street (established in 1870), Fashion Street (established in 1858) and Whites Row (established in 1860). These synagogues served the specific needs of Dutch, German and Polish migrants who initially chose to worship in *hevrot* either with their *landsleit* (countrymen) or with those in the same trade.

As immigrant arrivals increased, so the number of *hevrot* grew, providing a bridge with Eastern Europe, their names resonant of the old country even if their location was within the confines of London's East End. Grodno Synagogue was located in Spital Street, Kovno Synagogue in Catherine Wheel Alley and the Warsaw Synagogue in Gun Street. The *hevrot* varied in size and condition. Many were built on the backs of existing buildings or in converted, or operative, workshops.

Some, known as *stiebels*, consisted of just one room, often in a private house. For the male immigrant, both settled and more recently arrived, his *hevra* was far more than just a place of worship; it was almost a second home, a club and in some cases a friendly society which might provide benefits during sickness, unemployment and old age. It was a male meeting place where current political, social and economic issues could be debated, before, after and, frequently, during the service. Women were hidden from view, either by a curtain or in the gallery above.

Initially the small East End synagogues were independent both of the British Chief Rabbi and of each other. However, by the early 1880s concerns were being expressed about the 'undesirable' features of the *hevrot* and their impact on the image and structure of the Anglo-Jewish community. It was felt that there was a need to bring the disparate *hevrot* under some kind of control. Accordingly, in 1887, under the leadership of Samuel Montagu, at that time Liberal MP for Whitechapel and later 1st Lord Swaythling, the Federation of Synagogues was founded with an initial sixteen member synagogues. In 1889 the federation confirmed its autonomy through the purchase of a burial ground at Edmonton, north London.

Ten years later the building on the corner of Fournier Street and Brick Lane, which had originally been a Huguenot church, was bought by the ultra-Orthodox *Machzikei Hadath* and converted into a synagogue. It remained so until the early 1970s, when it was bought by the Bangladeshi community and converted into a mosque. This landmark building has come to represent the changing face of immigration and religion in the East End of London.

**RUSSIAN VAPOUR BATHS SIGN**
London, *c.*1900–14
Metal, enamel
0.6 x 1.2 m
Vapour baths were brought to England by immigrants from Russia and became part of social and religious life. Located on Brick Lane in the East End, these baths were run by Rev. Benjamin Schewzik, who also conducted Holy Day services at the Great Assembly Hall in Mile End.
2002.27

# CHARITY

The growth of the Jewish East End coincided with stagnation in the British economy. From the mid-1870s until almost the end of the first decade of the twentieth century, with just a brief respite between 1888 and 1892, Eastern European Jews, as well as non-Jews, experienced the hardships of under-employment and unemployment. Many were forced to turn to one of the numerous Jewish charities that had been established to ensure that poor Jews did not become a burden upon public funds. One of the most long-lived was the *Meshebat Nephesh* (Bread, Meat and Coal Society), established in 1779 in order to distribute bread, meat and coal to the London Jewish poor during the winter season. The society was still in existence 160 years later, providing for indigent Jews in the East End of London. By the time the Aliens Act was passed in 1905, restricting further immigration, there were more than forty Jewish philanthropic institutions and almost one hundred charities operating in London. Twelve societies gave assistance with food and fuel, and four distributed meals (though to different sections of the 'deserving' poor). There were also clothing societies and old people's homes, while between 1877 and 1897 the Jewish orphanage at Norwood more than doubled in size to meet the increase in need.

Though the charities sought to discourage the provision of welfare for newly arrived immigrants – the Jewish Board of Guardians would not provide for anyone who had been resident in England for less than six months – there were those who had compassion for the tired, hungry, scared and bedraggled arrivals. In 1884 a baker called Simon Cohen,

known as 'Simha Becker', opened a temporary shelter on his premises. Concern by members of the established Anglo-Jewish community led to its closure on the grounds that its facilities were 'unhealthy'. Following protests in 1885 a permanent Poor Jews' Temporary Shelter ws established in Leman Street, just to the south of Spitalfields, this time under the control of members of the Anglo-Jewish community. The shelter provided accommodation and meals for immigrants for up to two weeks, and its representatives met the new arrivals at the docks to protect them from exploitation. Many of those who passed through the shelter were transmigrants, a large number of whom, from the mid-1890s on, were in transit to South Africa. The Jewish Museum has a substantial collection of material relating to the Jews' Temporary Shelter, including photographs, the only known copy of the memoirs of Abraham Mundy, Secretary of the shelter from 1897 to 1940, and some poignant items left in its safe deposit boxes by those who passed through the shelter yet never reclaimed – a travelling jeweller's scales, rouble notes and some basic examples of ritual objects.

*Left:*
**JEWS' TEMPORARY SHELTER LIBRARY**
Isaac Perkoff, London, *c.*1906–14
Albumen print photograph
156 x 206 mm
Residents in the Library, or Reading Room, of the Jews' Temporary Shelter on Leman Street.
1988.507.8

*Above:*
**JEWELLER'S SCALES**
Eastern Europe, *c.*1885–1939
Brass, wood, metal, cotton thread
Case 24 x 132 x 64 mm
Balance scales and weights in a wooden case. One of a number of personal belongings left at the Jews' Temporary Shelter by residents, often as security for a small loan, but never collected.
1992.39.11

**DORA SHUSTER COLLECTING FOR
THE LONDON JEWISH HOSPITAL**
Isaac Perkoff, London, 1913
Hand-tinted gelatin silver print
photograph
712 x 437 mm
Dora Shuster is shown holding
a collecting box marked in
Yiddish 'Jewish Hospital Fund'.
Her parents were leading figures
in the establishment of the
hospital. As a schoolgirl Dora
worked as her father's
interpreter, secretary and book-
keeper. She later became known
as 'Lady Almoner' of the hospital
and was elected 'Founder and
Life Governor'.
1984.62

Many of the immigrants were also active in self-help initiatives, most notably friendly societies that, in return for weekly subscriptions, offered benefits to assist in times of sickness and death. In addition, they provided a sense of community and public life, with ceremonial regalia, well represented in the Museum's collections. In 1898 there were 150 Jewish benefit societies in the East End, and a survey in Spitalfields showed that between a half and two-thirds of adult males were members of one or more friendly societies. The London Jewish Hospital opened in 1919, funded through the pennies collected by the Jewish poor over twelve years.

**CLUPPER**, WITH OTHER TAILORING TOOLS
East London, *c.*1900–39
Wood
82 x 84 x 257 mm
A *clupper* (also known as a 'clapper') is a pounding block used by tailors to flatten parts of a garment: for example, a seam, pleat, dart or lapel. The photograph also shows other tools of the trade: a sleeve ironing board (1986.42.1), a wooden corner rule (1997.14.5.2), a box of thimbles and a piece of cloth (1987.133).
1985.105.3

# ECONOMIC ACTIVITY

The East End of London, on the periphery of the City and close to the more affluent West End, was where most of the immigrants sought employment. When available, work was for the most part seasonal and subject to the vagaries of the economy and public demand. For those prepared to work long hours, in the worst conditions, for the lowest pay, in other words as sweated labour, there was employment. It was in the clothing trade that most work was found. It is estimated that five-sevenths of male immigrants from Eastern Europe worked in the Jewish-run ready-to-wear tailoring workshops that were burgeoning all over the East End. In unsanitary conditions in workshops that were built on the backs of terraced houses, or in unhealthy basements or attics, tailors, machiners, plain-machiners, pressers and under-pressers toiled away for long hours in the busy times and hung around for work in the slack. Many of those employed in the trade were unskilled 'greeners', recruited straight from the docks on disembarkation.

Women too contributed to the household economy, often working in tailoring or cigarette-making workshops when single, and, following marriage, running small shops, taking in lodgers or assisting in their husbands' tailoring workshops as unpaid hands, helping out in the busy season and making do in the slack.

All but the most fortunate and skilled of the tailoring workers suffered from the inequity of long hours and low pay. One response was the formation of specifically Jewish trade unions. Between 1872 and 1914 fifty-two Jewish tailoring trade unions were founded. However, the majority proved ephemeral and ineffective. In 1889, and again in 1912, the Jewish tailoring workers of London held large-scale strikes in an attempt to force their co-religionist employers to improve working conditions. However, these proved largely unsuccessful, for, even though concessions were made, it took only a few weeks for the employers to go back on their word. While there was a continuing stream of newcomers, exploitation would remain a fact of life.

The situation differed little in the other immigrant trades. Jewish workers found employment as boot- and slipper-makers, cabinetmakers, cigarette-makers and furriers. By 1901 about

**JEWISH TAILORS' WORKSHOP**
London, c.1925–29
Photograph
104 x 153 mm
Ladies' tailors workshop in Commercial Road in the East End of London. In the centre is Rose Kosky (*née* Markovitch), who came to England from Poland with her three brothers.
68.1

10 per cent of British Jews were working in the furniture trade, and many small furniture firms were set up in the Curtain Road area, alongside the timberyards and trade mills. Other immigrants worked in trades serving their co-religionists as shopkeepers, bakers and *kosher* butchers. In the years before 1914 only a few of the immigrants made it out of the Jewish East End, as traditional small-scale industries began to grow. The ready-to-wear clothing industry developed in newer, larger factories, and by 1907 the Lebus furniture factory employed almost 4,000 workers on a new site in Tottenham in north London. Following the First World War, conditions started to improve and Jewish people began to enter a wider range of occupations, such as hairdressing, retail and taxi driving.

*Right:*

**TIMBERYARD**

L. & J. Suss photographic studios, London, *c.*1895
Albumen print photograph
149 x 102 mm
Timber merchant Arnold Herman Barmaper, who came to England from Austria, with staff in his timberyard in Bethnal Green, east London.
1990.157.9

*Left:*

**WOODWORKING TOOLS**

Nineteenth or early twentieth century
Wood and metal
Miscellaneous woodworking instruments used in the cabinet-making industry
1986.138

# CULTURAL AND SOCIAL LIFE

Life, though hard, was not without its brighter side. Yiddish theatre provided one cultural outlet. The first professional Yiddish actors arrived in the East End in 1883, and Yiddish theatre reached its peak in the first decades of the twentieth century. It embraced a repertoire that covered traditional Eastern European drama through to the equivalent of rowdy East End music hall. Also featured were Yiddish translations of classics by Shakespeare and Ibsen, as well as specially written plays which portrayed the immigrant experience in England, and even opera. The Museum's rich collection of material relating to Yiddish theatre includes posters, programmes and photographs of the stars of the Yiddish stage, as well as costumes from some of the last performers.

Also popular were Schewzik's Vapour Baths in Brick Lane, a local landmark whose sign proclaimed 'Best Massage in London: Invaluable relief for Rheumatism, Gout, Sciatica, Neuritis, Lumbago and Allied Complaints. Keep fit and well by regular visits' (see p.148). Vapour baths were particularly popular with men, who would go there after work before going to synagogue for Friday night prayers.

Throughout the lifetime of the Jewish East End, there was a buoyant Yiddish press which covered the political spectrum from moderate to anarchist, the latter accommodated by *Der Arbeiter Fraint*, which appeared intermittently between 1885 and 1910, and the short-lived *Polishe Yidel*. Other less extreme journals such as the *Yidisher Telefon, Yidisher Velt, Die Yiddishe Stimme* and *Yidisher Zhurnal* provided local and national news and gossip, thus building bridges between the immigrants and the English way of life.

Another important element in political and social life was the Workers' Circle, a socialist Jewish friendly society. Founded in 1903 at the instigation of *Arbeiter Fraint*, it continued in existence until the 1980s. While it dispensed with the regalia associated with other friendly societies, it offered members cultural activities such as lectures and concerts, a library and a Yiddish school. The Jewish Museum holds a substantial quantity of documentary material relating to the Workers' Circle.

*Opposite:*
**POSTER FOR 'THE EMINENT TRAGEDIAN JOSEPH KESSLER'**
Commissioned by Harry H. Krone, London, *c.*1913–25
Theatre poster showing the Hungarian-born actor Joseph Kessler, with vignettes of the actor in Shakespearean roles. Kessler was an important figure in Yiddish theatre in both New York and London, specialising in Shakespeare tragedies and the literary classics of the Yiddish repertoire.
513.9

*Left:*
**THE KING OF LAMPEDUSA**
London, 1944
Photograph
Actors Meier Tzelniker, Anna Tzelniker and Clara Meisels in a performance of *The King of Lampedusa*. This was the longest-running Yiddish play in London, based on the true story of RAF Flight Sergeant Sydney Cohen, who single-handedly took the Italian island of Lampedusa.
500.55

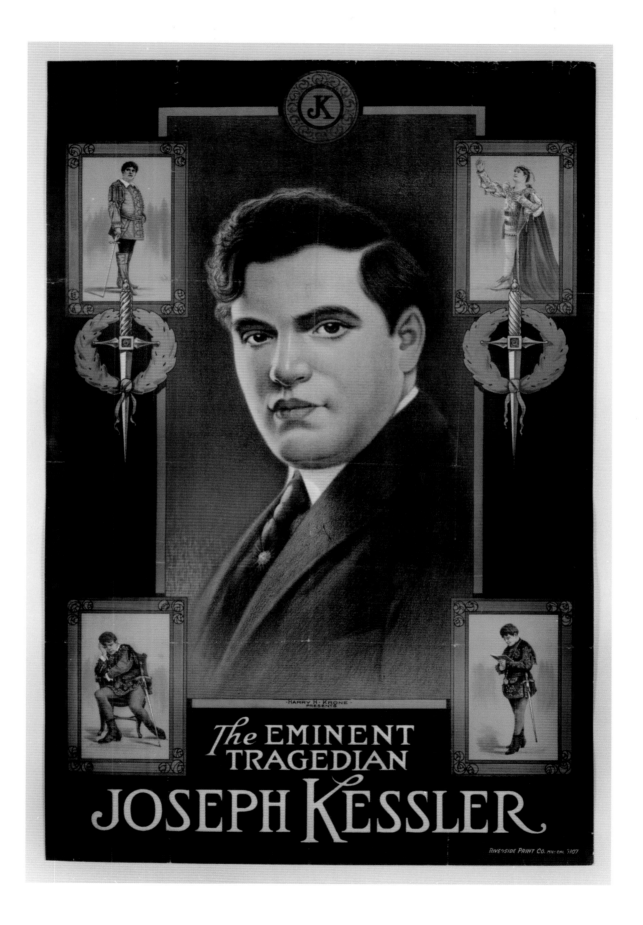

*JEWS' FREE SCHOOL:*
*PLAYGROUND ASSEMBLY*
London, 1908
Sepia photograph
240 x 296 mm
Pupils and teachers of the
school assemble in the
playground.
E 1991.124

Education was of primary importance for children growing up in the Jewish East End. In addition to the local board schools – by the 1890s Christ Church School in Brick Lane had a pupil body which was 95 per cent Jewish – there was the Jews' Free School. Founded in 1817, by the end of the nineteenth century it was one of the largest schools in Europe. At its location in Bell Lane, in the heart of Spitalfields, it accommodated over 4,000 pupils (E 1991.124).

By the close of the nineteenth century the Jewish community had acquired a reputation for the regularity of its children's school attendance. In addition, many children attended *heder* (religion classes) and recreational clubs such as the Oxford and St George's and the Brady Boys' and Girls' Clubs, both well represented in the Museum's collections. The Jewish Lads' Brigade was founded in an attempt to 'iron out the ghetto bend' and to transform the children of immigrants into 'Englishmen of the Mosaic persuasion'. Companies of the brigade were formed in other parts of the country, wherever there were immigrant working-class neighbourhoods. Military-style uniform and training aimed to 'instil into the rising

generation, from earliest youth, habits of orderliness, cleanliness and honour, so that in learning to respect themselves they will do credit to their Community'. One of the high spots of brigade life was the annual summer camp, which for many of those attending was their first sight of the sea and a rural landscape.

Life in the Jewish East End was a mixture of hardship and happiness, of neighbourliness and exploitation. While for many of the elder immigrants it was a terminal, for their children it was a launching pad to a more successful future (118.1). The movement out of the East End began during the First World War and accelerated in the 1920s and 1930s as new suburbs developed in London to the north, north-east and north-west. The end of the Jewish East End as a thriving centre of Jewish life came with the Second World War, when the Blitz forced many away. By the 1960s there remained only a residual, mainly elderly, community, and the crowded and jostling streets and lanes of the Jewish East End became just a memory. The area in and around Spitalfields was soon to become home to new immigrants arriving from Bangladesh, and by the 1990s it would be known as 'Banglatown'.

**KRAVITZ WEDDING PORTRAIT**
Boris Bennett, London,
8 August 1937
Photograph
Studio portrait of Debbie and
Hymie Kravitz on their wedding
day, by the popular studio
photographer known as 'Boris',
who operated in London
throughout the 1930s and 1940s,
photographing hundreds of East
End couples. Mr Kravitz's family
came to England from Poland,
and he worked in the furniture
trade. The couple were married
at Harley Street Synagogue,
Bow, and the reception was at
the Imperial Ballrooms, Mile
End. Most of the bridal couples
photographed by Boris would
soon leave the East End for the
suburbs.
118.1

# REFUGEES FROM NAZISM

Martin Gilbert

The story of Britain and the refugees from Nazism is a
remarkable one. Britain provided a safe haven to more than
60,000 German, Austrian and Czech Jewish refugees before
the borders of Germany were sealed at the outbreak of war.
At the time of greatest need the British government and
British Jewry made the greatest effort.

# BEFORE THE SECOND WORLD WAR

Britain opened its doors from the first days of Hitler's coming to power in Germany in January 1933. In the period between *Kristallnacht* in November 1938 and the outbreak of the Second World War in September 1939 the United States gave refuge to 500 Jewish youngsters. In that same period Britain took in almost 10,000. Later, in May 1945, after the defeat of Hitler and Nazism, Britain was to give sanctuary to the survivors of the Holocaust.

Among the refugees who came after 1933 were some who made an astonishing contribution to British life and to British wartime preparedness and efficiency. Viennese-born Professor Abel pioneered the adaptation of dry batteries with the raw materials available in wartime, to meet the special requirements of the fighting forces. Also from Vienna, Professor Gross pioneered work on aluminium bronzes that made a major contribution to the wartime production of aircraft and of ships' propellers. Berlin-born Professor Ernst Chain isolated and purified penicillin in time for it to be used to save innumerable lives on the battlefield, and ever since.

All this is documented in the collections of the Jewish Museum. The archives are a rich repository of the refugee story. The documents and objects make it possible to learn about the whole saga of rescue, from 1933 to 1945, and to follow it on an almost daily basis, not only through statistics and the politics of rescue – which are important – but also through the stories of individuals.

It is these personal stories and testimonies that give a human face to the suffering, and to the rejoicing, of those whose fate was in the balance. Where the British politicians hesitated, where British newspapers tried to whip up popular anti-refugee prejudice, they tell that story too.

Again and again men and women of goodwill triumphed over prejudice and negativity. After 1933 many British schools made a particular effort to take in Jewish refugees. One such school was King's College, Taunton. It offered reduced fees to schoolboys fleeing Nazi persecution. One of those boys was Kurt Abrahamson (who later took the name Ken Ambrose). His story is illustrated in the Museum. He was from the German Baltic port of Stettin, and entered King's College in January 1936. In the summer of 1938 he was school vice-captain; the Museum holds a number of house notices written in this capacity (for example, 2004.5.3.4). Also in the Museum's collections are the camera he brought with him in 1936 (2004.5.2), which had been given to him as a *Barmitzvah* present four years earlier, and his typewriter (2004.5.1), received on the same occasion.

**TYPED NOTICE**
Kenneth Ambrose, Taunton,
3 May 1938
Paper
98 x 156 mm
Notice reminding pupils at King's College, Taunton, that they must sit in their allotted seats at mealtimes. Signed in ink 'K. A.'. Typed on the typewriter that Ambrose brought with him from Germany in 1936.
2004.5.3.4

The seating for breakfast, tea and supper must be strictly adhered to. If a boy finds that no place is laid for him where he ought to sit, he must not sit in another boy's place but must ask a waiter to lay a place for him and bring a chair.in his proper place. Mr. Cheter-Master is very particular about this matter and will interfere if any more persons are found in the wrong places.

3/5/38.

K. A.

Toad in the hole — Kröte in der Höhle (ein sehr beliebtes Fleisch-gericht).

Eine Rumpsteakschnitte wird in Streifen geschnitten, eventuell auch eine Schafsniere, gesalzen, gepfeffert, in eine ausgefettete feuer-feste Schüssel arrangiert, ein Teig wie unter yorkshire pudding ange-geben darübergegossen und ca. 1½ Stunden im Rohr gebacken. Ser-vieren mit Bratensaft.

**Bubble and squeak.**

Dünne Schnitten von kaltem, gekochten Rindfleisch werden in etwas Butter angebraten (nicht austrocknen lassen) und lagenweise mit Grüngemüse in eine Schüssel geschichtet und serviert.

Grüngemüse dazu:

Kraut, Kohlsprößen oder Wirsingkohl wird gekocht, abgeseiht, fein gehackt und mit einer geschnittenen Zwiebel, Salz und Pfeffer in heißem Fett eine Zeit lang gebraten.

**Beef roll — Rindfleisch-Roulade.**

Gekochte oder gebratene Reste von Rindfleisch werden faschiert, gut gewürzt, eventuell etwas Fett zugefügt. Butterteig wird dünn aus-gewalkt, die Fleischfarce eingefüllt, zu einer Rolle geformt und in heißem Rohr eine halbe Stunde gebacken.

Derart können auch kleine Täschchen geformt werden.

**Beef rissoles — Rindfleisch-Croquetten.**

1 lb Roastbeef (gebraten) wird faschiert, ¼ lb Brösel, etwas Fett, 2 Eier, Salz, Pfeffer, Zwiebel, Thymian, Zitronenschalen etc. hinzu-gefügt, gut abgemischt, Croquettes geformt, in Ei und Brösel paniert und in heißem Fett ausgebacken.

**Shepherds pie — Schäferpastete.**

½ lb dünn aufgeschnittener Hammelbraten, 1 lb gekochte passierte Kartoffel, 1 oz Butter, Salz, Pfeffer, feingehackte Zwiebel, ½ pint gravy oder stock.

Die passierten Kartoffel werden mit Butter, Salz, Pfeffer, eventuell Muskat vermischt und in einer Pfanne auf Feuer abgeröstet. Man fettet eine feuerfeste Schüssel, gibt die Hälfte der Kartoffeln hinein, darüber das Fleisch, zwischen jede Lage etwas Salz, Pfeffer und fein-gehackte Zwiebel, übergießt das Ganze mit Bratensaft oder Suppe, streicht die zweite Hälfte der Kartoffel darüber, setzt einige Butter-flöckchen obenauf und bäckt es im Rohr bis die Decke braun und knusprig ist.

**Poor man's goose — Arme-Leute-Gans.**

³⁄₄ lb Schweinsleber, ¼ lb Speck, 1 Ei, Brösel.

Die Leber schaben, den Speck in kleine Würfel schneiden, mit einer feingehackten Zwiebel in eine Kasserolle auf Feuer setzen und

20

Kurt Abrahamson came to Britain by himself. The story of his family is an illustration of Britain's response to the persecutions in Germany. During the destruction of *Kristallnacht* in November 1938 his father was one of 30,000 German Jews taken to concentration camps in Germany. After English friends acted as guarantors, he was released, and in April 1939 came to Britain with his wife and daughter, who found employment as a domestic. Thus the family was reunited.

In 1934, within two years of Hitler's coming to power, a school for German-Jewish refugees was established at Stoatley Rough, near Haslemere in Surrey. The board of governors was headed by a distinguished Quaker, Bertha Bracey, who was extremely active in refugee matters. The German annexation of Austria in March 1938 led to an influx of Austrian Jewish children – they were known in the school, affectionately, as the 'Austrian invaders'. The Museum has an evocative collection of reminiscences about Stoatley Rough School (1994.71.1 & 2, 1995.11).

The Museum archives also contain the history of a hostel for refugees opened by a Jewish paediatrician, Dr Bernard Schlesinger, in Shepherd's Hill, Highgate (2000.12). The account shows how hard Schlesinger had to work to open the hostel, and to get local government permission. He persevered, and he succeeded. As well as taking in the young refugees, Schlesinger also saved four German-Jewish women by acquiring permits for them to come to Britain, one to be matron in the hostel and the three others to look after the children, to do the cooking and the office work.

There was more to refuge than a safe haven. Life had to go on, and the rich heritage of German-Jewish life in all its aspects could not be pushed aside. At the same time the local customs and way of life had to be tackled. A recipe book, in German, contains favourite English recipes for immigrant cooks (1998.62.5).

Artefacts form a fascinating visual aspect of the refugee story. There is a large travelling trunk, more like a wardrobe, brilliantly arranged, which belonged to the Kohnstamm family (1997.3). Its many compartments, compact and skilfully designed, enabled the family to bring at least some of their clothes in an ordered fashion.

**TRUNK**
Mädler Koffer, Germany, *c*.1930
Leather, cloth, metal, wood
1.30 x 0.54 x 0.46 m
Trunk used by the Kohnstamm
family, German refugees, on
their journey to England.
1997.3

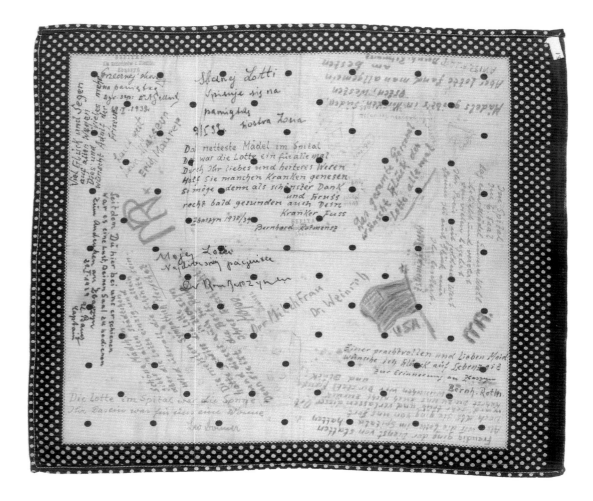

**HANDKERCHIEF COVERED IN MESSAGES**

Zbaszyn, Poland, 1938–39
Cotton
370 x 425 mm
This handkerchief was brought
to England by Lotte Frankel
from Zbaszyn, a camp for Polish
Jews who had been expelled
from Germany in 1938. It is
signed with goodbyes and good
luck messages from other camp
inmates.
2000.5.1

Towards the end of October 1938 the Nazi authorities expelled 15,000 German Jews and dumped them on the Polish border. At first the Poles were reluctant to give them refuge. Some of these deportees had been born in Poland but had lived for ten, twenty, even thirty years in Germany. Their German-born children were deported with them. One of these youngsters, Lotte Frankel, spent seven months at the Polish border. Her story is told at the Museum. In May 1939 she was able to come to Britain on a student permit, bringing with her a handkerchief covered in messages from her fellow inmates at Zbaszyn refugee camp (2000.5.1). After the outbreak of war her parents were sent to the Lodz Ghetto. From Lodz her mother was later deported to Auschwitz and killed.

On 7 November 1938 in Paris a young Jew, distraught at the plight of his parents, who had been deported to the Polish border two weeks earlier, shot and killed a German diplomat. Using this as an excuse, on the night of 9/10 November the Nazi regime launched an orgy of destruction against the Jews of Germany and Austria. During what is known as *Kristallnacht* ('the Night of Broken Glass') several hundred synagogues were destroyed, several thousand Jewish shops were looted and vandalised, and several hundred Jews killed, on the night itself and after the mass deportation to concentration camps on the following day.

Among the powerful testimonies in the Museum is that of a thirteen-year-old Jewish boy who recalled how, on 10 November, 'when I arrived at my school I saw the Swastika flag on the roof. All the school windows were broken and the portrait of the man who founded the school was lying in the street. There were no lessons that day. I walked home. Some boys threw stones at me. At about midnight a Gestapo and an SS-man came to our house and said to father, "Dress yourself and come with me."'

One of the moving documents in the Museum archives is the order of service of a service of prayer and intercession for the Jews of Germany, held on 20 November 1938 in response to *Kristallnacht* (2002.3.1). It was printed by the office of the Chief Rabbi. One prayer recited that day was addressed to Germany: 'Man is brought low; human brotherhood is become a mockery; and there is neither truth, pity nor freedom in the land. And they have set their face utterly to defame and destroy the House of Israel.'

In response to the outrages of *Kristallnacht*, the British government offered to take in 10,000 Jewish children without the formalities of applications and visas. This became known as the 'Kindertransport'. The children who came to Britain with it are known as the *Kinder*. The first children, 206 orphans and children whose fathers had been deported to concentration camps on 10 November, arrived at Parkeston Quay, Harwich, on 2 December 1938.

The Museum holds several examples of the documents carried by the *Kinder*. One of them states: 'This document of identity is issued with the approval of His Majesty's Government … to young persons to be admitted to the United Kingdom for educational purposes … The document requires no visa' (1993.74.3).

The stories of the *Kinder* are thoroughly represented in the Museum. So too are stories relating to the reception of the newcomers, as well as the more than 8,000 adults who were admitted between *Kristallnacht* and the outbreak of war. Among the many documents are those that relate to the Co-ordinating Committee for Refugees, licensed by the London County Council to operate a domestic bureau, through which adult Jews could apply from Germany for positions as domestics, and, when accepted, get the documents needed to come to Britain.

Letters and other documents in the Museum's collection show the goodwill of those many non-Jews who were eager to help. Mrs M. E. Raven, of the Prior's House, Ely, Cambridgeshire, offered a housekeeping job to Gertrud Landshoff, whose husband had died and who, in the immediate aftermath of *Kristallnacht*, had simply written 'It has become necessary for me to emigrate' (1995.20). Filling in the Domestic Bureau Enquiry Request Form on 16 February 1939, William J. Chalk states simply, about a Jewish would-be refugee from Germany 'I want to employ her' (1990.68.16).

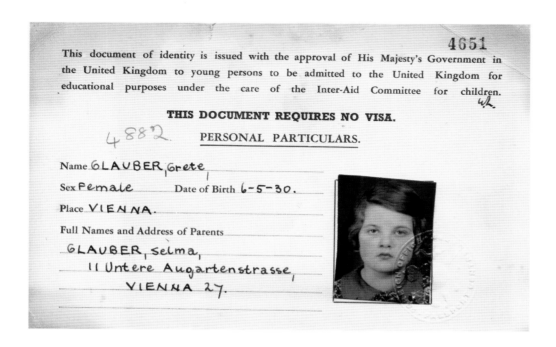

**IDENTITY CARD FOR GRETE GLAUBER**
Inter-Aid Committee for Children from Germany, 1939
Paper
126 x 202 mm
Card carried by Grete Glauber during her journey to England on the Kindertransport.
1993.74.3

That was enough. Another life was saved. Among the artefacts in the Museum is a white apron used by one such domestic servant (1988.56).

Those who had been rescued were swift to say thank you. This can be seen in the scroll of appreciation given to Mr and Mrs Bond, the managers of Dovercourt Bay holiday camp, used as a reception centre for the *Kinder*. It is illustrated and signed by 'the German refugee children' and the staff (1998.92). It is dated 29 March 1939, when the Kindertransport children were still arriving in Britain every few days.

Those who helped bring the *Kinder* to Britain are also well represented at the Museum. Among them were Nicholas Winton and his close associate Trevor Chadwick, a Latin teacher from Swanage in Dorset. Travelling to Prague after the German occupation of the city in March 1939, Chadwick provided counterfeit papers for those children who did not have the proper travel documents, and, when challenged at the border, persuaded the German authorities to allow the children to continue to Britain.

One of the children helped by Winton and Chadwick was seventeen-year-old Margit Freudenbergová, some of whose documents are housed in the Museum (E 947.1 & 2). She was number 159 on the list of her particular Kindertransport. Her train left Masaryk Station in Prague at 1.30 p.m. on 31 May 1939, and her journey took her through Germany and the Netherlands, across the North Sea to Harwich, and on by rail from Harwich to London and then Glasgow.

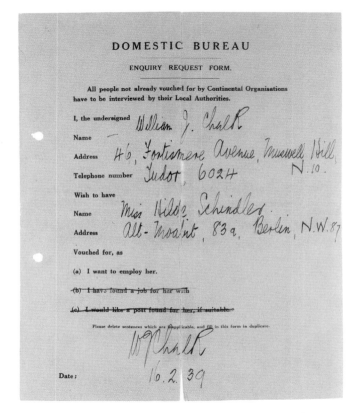

*Below:*
**POUCH OF DOCUMENTS**
Karlsruhe, 1939
Linen, card
115 x 120 mm
Linen pouch containing a photograph, instructions and entry documentation, brought by Richard Kaufmann when he came to Britain on the Kindertransport, aged twelve. It was made for him by his mother.
E 966

*Above:*
**DOMESTIC BUREAU ENQUIRY REQUEST FORM**
Domestic Bureau/William J. Chalk, London,
16 February 1939
Paper
255 x 203 mm
Form requesting that inquiries be made about Hilde Schindler, a German-Jewish refugee seeking employment.
1990.68.16

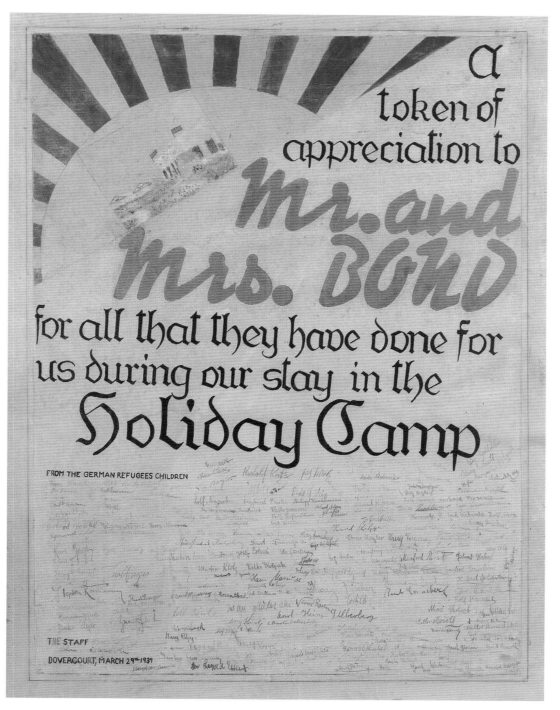

**DOVERCOURT BAY KINDERTRANSPORT SCROLL**
Dovercourt Bay holiday camp, 29 March 1939
Paper
935 x 737 mm
In December 1938 Dovercourt Bay Holiday Camp, near Harwich, found a new use as a reception centre for Kindertransport arrivals.
1998.92

One unusual item gives a flavour of the perils of the *Kinder*'s journey. It is the small linen pouch carried on his journey by twelve-year-old Richard Kaufmann, from the German city of Karlsruhe (E 966). Travelling by himself, he made the journey as far as Rotterdam, via Paris and Brussels. In the pouch are small index cards on which he had been given instructions about the precise timings of the trains and the towns through which he would pass, as well as directions he might need to ask in French.

A significant historical document in the Museum's collection is a German passport with a Bolivian visa, which enabled its holder to leave Berlin for South America (E 1568.1). Another is an official British parliamentary publication, issued in 1939, giving in stark detail the accounts by the British consuls in Germany of the persecution of the Jews at the time of *Kristallnacht* (1991.72).

The suitcase of fifteen-year-old Martin Thau from Berlin, containing a change of clothes, writing materials, a *tallit* and *tefillin* and family photographs, can also be found in the collections (1992.47). Martin arrived at Harwich on 26 July 1939. His sister and stepmother were to follow in a few months. Germany invaded Poland on 1 September 1939, and Britain declared war on Germany three days later. War had broken out before their permits could arrive. Neither survived the war.

Some would-be *Kinder* were already in the neutral Netherlands when war broke out, and were able to continue their journey. The last journey was in May 1940, a few days after Germany violated Dutch neutrality and forced the Dutch to surrender.

**'HOMELESS' SONGSHEET**
Curt Wolf and Martin Mayne,
Isle of Man, 1940
Paper
148 x 210 mm
Song on being a refugee,
addressed from the internment
camp, Isle of Man.
1988.567.53

# DURING THE SECOND WORLD WAR

Later that month, as German forces conquered Belgium and France in addition to the Netherlands, the British government, fearful of a German Fifth Column such as had helped the German invaders in the Netherlands, rounded up large numbers of 'enemy aliens' and interned them. Most were interned on the Isle of Man. Many of these 'enemy aliens' were Jewish refugees who had arrived from Germany the previous year. This aspect of the refugee story is also portrayed at the Museum, with collections including a songsheet entitled 'Homeless', written on the Isle of Man (1988.567.53).

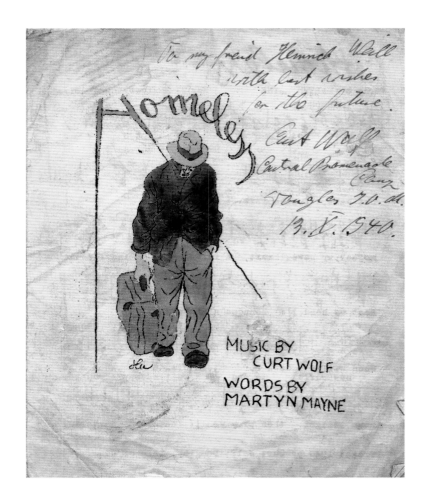

Many of those who were interned on the Isle of Man later volunteered for service in the British Army. Earlier refugees from Germany also served with distinction alongside British Jews. Their war service was on many fronts and in many branches of national defence. The Museum's material includes several impressive stories. Two of them will give a sense of the collection.

The first soldier, Erhard Stern (who became known as Edward), a dentist, came to Britain from Germany in 1935. When war came he wanted to become an airman, but as a German national was refused admission to the Royal Air Force. On 26 February 1940 he joined the Pioneer Corps. Three months later he was on the beaches of Dunkirk, one of the hundreds of thousands of British soldiers being evacuated as the German Army tried to drive them into the sea. Joining the Army Dental Corps, he was a pioneer of army dental studies (2003.7).

The second soldier, Bernhard Tuchmann, was born in Vienna in 1924. The records at the Museum (E 1893) show that he reached Harwich with a Kindertransport on 23 December 1938. He was then fourteen years old. In the spring of 1944, just after his twentieth birthday, he was in uniform. In December 1944 he was killed in action in France.

**'THE BOYS' IN PRAGUE**
Prague, 9 August 1945
Photograph
Some 300 Jewish children,
survivors of the Holocaust,
gathered in the Old Town
Square in Prague before
departing for England.
1118.2

# AFTER THE SECOND WORLD WAR

Immediately after the defeat of Germany in May 1945 the British government arranged for more than 700 teenage concentration camp survivors who had been liberated from Theresienstadt to be flown to Britain. The group became known as 'The Boys', although there were some girls among them. Once in Britain they were rehabilitated at a camp at Windermere in the Lake District and then dispersed to schools and hostels throughout Britain. Their story forms part of the Museum's collection, which includes photographs of them in Prague after liberation (1118.2), watching a film at their hostel in Windermere (1141.4) and playing football, once they had come to London and formed their own sports and social club, the Primrose Club (1120.7).

**PRIMROSE CLUB FOOTBALL TEAM**
London, *c.*1948
Photograph
1120.7

*Above:*
**TOY TRUCK**
Netherlands, *c.*1940
Wood
85 x 355 x 80 mm
This toy was made by Leon Greenman
for his son, who was murdered in
Auschwitz at the age of two. LMS
stands for London Midlands Scottish
Railways, chosen deliberately to show
support for Britain.
T 128

Also reaching Britain after the war was Leon Greenman.
Born in Whitechapel, in the heart of the East End, in 1910, he
was living in the Netherlands when war came. Despite being
a British citizen, he was deported from the Netherlands to
Auschwitz and later to Buchenwald. In November 1945 he
arrived back in Britain. His collection of memorabilia is an
important one. Most poignant are the objects relating to his
son Barney, who was killed at Auschwitz, along with Leon's
wife, Else. This includes the young boy's tin moneybox (T 127),
his wooden toy (T 128), his shoes (T 120) and a framed lock
of his hair (T 121). As well as images of Barney (for example
1056.1), the photographs in the Museum's collection illustrate
the thriving Jewish community of Rotterdam before the
Holocaust, and also Leon's recovery after liberation at
Buchenwald (for example, 533.7).

*Left:*
**SHOES**
Netherlands, *c.*1941–42
Leather, rubber
Each shoe 60 x 150 x 65 mm
Pair of brown leather shoes
belonging to Barney Greenman.
The soles were repaired by
his father, Leon, using layers
of rubber from a tyre.
T 120

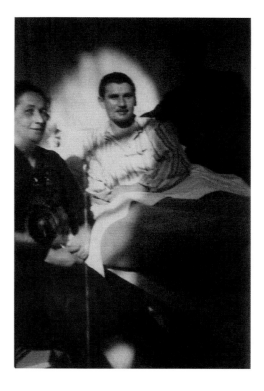

Most of the Kindertransport children never saw their
parents again after saying goodbye to them at the railway
station in Germany, Austria or Czechoslovakia where they
began their journey to Britain. Among the Museum's stories,
however, is one with a happy ending. Lily Fischl had sent her
two sons to Britain in 1939. She herself was later deported to
Theresienstadt and then to a slave labour camp at Oederan;
while in the camps she made a wooden toothbrush for herself
(1990.207), poignant evidence of the daily struggle of camp
life. She survived and was reunited with her sons in Britain in
1946, seven years after they had said their farewells.

One contemporary source, in response to criticism that the
needs of the Kindertransport children were not always perfectly
understood or catered for, replied: 'In an ideal world we would
have checked the needs of the children and matched them
with carefully compiled family profiles, but in an ideal world,
refugee children would not have existed.'

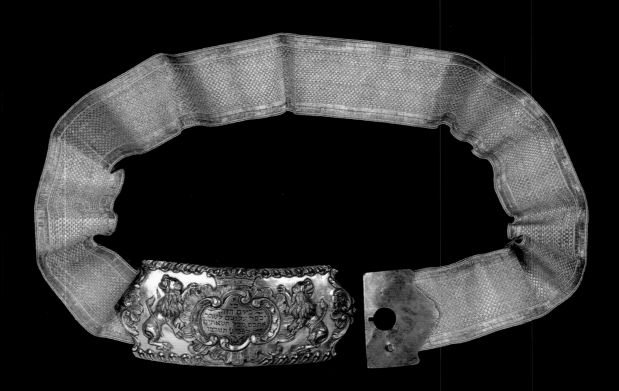

# FROM DIVERSE LANDS

Rickie Burman and Lily Steadman

Since Cromwell's readmission of Jews to England in 1656, the
British Jewish community has absorbed immigrants and
influences from all over the world, reflecting Britain's role and
importance on the international stage, including colonialism
and Empire. The cultural backgrounds and experiences of
these diverse groups, reflected within the Jewish community
today, are represented in many areas of the Jewish Museum's
collections, including photographs, prints, ceremonial art and
social history material.

The first settlers to establish themselves in seventeenth-century London were Sephardi Jews, descendants of those who had been expelled from Spain and Portugal at the end of the fifteenth century. When the Dutch Prince William of Orange became King of England in 1688, they were joined by a steady flow of people from Amsterdam, and at the end of the seventeenth century the first Ashkenazi Jews began to arrive from Central and Eastern Europe. The population continued to grow, and by the late nineteenth century there were about 65,000 Jewish people in Britain – a substantial community within which modern migrants have found their own place.

Following their expulsion from the Iberian peninsula, Sephardi Jews settled in north Africa, in north-west Europe – particularly the Netherlands, famous for its climate of religious tolerance – and in the Ottoman Empire, which included the Balkans and most of Hungary. They brought with them Ladino, a language combining elements of medieval Spanish and Hebrew. In Britain, as elsewhere, they were the dominant force in the Jewish community in the seventeenth and eighteenth centuries.

Despite arriving in this country much later than the Sephardim, the Ashkenazim came to comprise the majority of British Jews. Their name derives from the medieval Hebrew word *Ashkenaz*, meaning 'Germany'. This reflects the fact that the medieval forebears of the modern Ashkenazim lived in the German-speaking lands of Central Europe. They were expelled in the fourteenth century, moving east into Russia and Galicia, and taking with them the Yiddish language, which has a

German base but incorporates many words from Hebrew. Yiddish remained the language of the Jews of Eastern Europe for the next 500 years and was their mother tongue well into the twentieth century. The survival of the language was a crucial factor in the development of a self-contained Jewish culture in Russia and Poland, including thriving religious scholarship and literature.

Despite their diverse origins, there are strong similarities in the objects that Jewish immigrants from different parts of the world chose to bring with them, examples of which now form a significant part of the collections of the Jewish Museum. Of central importance are objects associated with religious life; the ubiquity of items such as spice boxes and *kippot* (head coverings) reminds us that, although they came from widely varying cultures, all these individuals were united by their faith. The materials and decoration of ritual objects may be influenced by their place of origin, yet their common function reflects the shared heritage of Jewish religious practice around the world.

The second major category of objects is personal effects – items such as clothes, household items and mementoes of home, often regarded as the essentials for someone starting a new life in a foreign country. The overall picture, therefore, is of a group of objects which, while differing in their design according to their place of origin, are very similar in their more fundamental characteristics.

*Opposite:*
**YOM KIPPUR BELT**
Lvov, 1790
Silver, silver gilt, niello, satin
Buckle 71 x 169 mm, belt 824 mm long
Belt of woven satin in a chequered pattern. Buckle of silver and silver gilt with a niello inscription in Hebrew. Repoussé decoration of lions rampant, holding an ornate cartouche with the inscription, surmounted by a crown. The belt was brought to England from the Ukraine, via Austria.
C 1981.4.13.3

*Right:*
**KIPPAH**
Germany (?), *c.*1900–39
Silk, metal thread
110 x 180 mm
Cream-coloured silk *kippah* gathered at the top to create a dome shape. Border and top piece embroidered in silver-coloured metallic thread with stylised flowers, leaves and branches. Brought to England by Mrs K. Suessman, who fled from Breslau in Germany (now Wroclaw in Poland) to England in the early 1940s.
1987.114

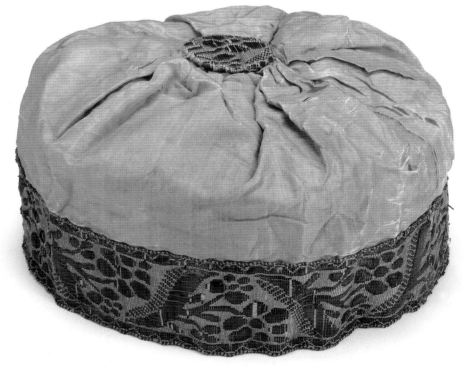

*Right:*
**POLISH WOMAN**

N. J. Juress, Poland, *c.*1890–1905
Photograph
150 x 105 mm
Studio portrait of the Polish-Jewish woman who owned the bonnet shown below. In this photograph she wears it over a wig or *sheitel*.
103.7

*Right:*
**WOMAN'S BONNET**

Poland, *c.*1890–1905
Silk, lace, velvet, wire, sequins, feathers
265 mm high (without feathers); 270 mm wide (at widest point)
Black bonnet decorated with artificial flowers, sequins and feathers. This bonnet was brought to Britain by a Polish-Jewish immigrant who eventually settled in Wales.
1986.135.7

# THE GREAT MIGRATION

From the 1880s until the early part of the twentieth century there was a substantial increase in Jewish immigration to Britain from Eastern Europe. About 150,000 Jewish people arrived in Britain between 1881 and 1914, fleeing the pogroms and persecution in Russia and Poland. Among the objects in the Museum's collection from this period of migration is an elaborate bonnet (1986.135.7), whose owner came from the village of Nowy Dwor in Poland and settled in Wales at the turn of the century.

She can be seen wearing it over her *sheitel* (the wig traditionally worn by very observant Jewish women following marriage) in a studio photograph (103.7) taken in Poland and kept as a reminder of her former life. The bonnet is decorated with feathers, lace, ribbon bows, sequins sewn on in the shapes of birds, and velvet flowers, leaves, stems and buds. Both bonnet and photograph illustrate the importance for these new immigrants of making a good impression and keeping up their high standards, despite the difficulties of their situation. Likewise, continuity with life before migration is shown by the fact that another woman brought a heavy *lokshen*-making machine (1985.171) so that she could make traditional noodles in her new home. A more common item is the pestle and mortar (1992.31) brought from Latvia.

*Above:*
**PESTLE AND MORTAR**
Latvia, *c*.1830–98
Brass
Mortar 117 x 129 mm;
pestle 217 mm long
Pestle with flat button-shaped ends, and vase-shaped mortar. Brought to England by a woman who came from Riga, Latvia, in about 1898.
1992.31

*Below:*
***LOKSHEN*-MAKING MACHINE**
Europe, *c*.1875–1900
Wood, metal
200 x 112 x 229 mm (when closed)
*Lokshen* is the Yiddish name for thin noodles similar to vermicelli. They are traditionally put into soup, or made into a sweet baked *lokshen* pudding with eggs, sugar, raisins and spices.
1985.171

One Polish family arriving in about 1880 brought with them a delicate Passover tea service (1998.33); it has fine gold decoration on a pale pink and white ground. Following their arrival in England, the family bought several replica pieces to replace breakages to the original service, again demonstrating the value attached by the immigrants to these items from *der heim*. It is often through such domestic objects that we can see most clearly into the lives of the immigrants – although far from home, they worked to build ordinary lives for themselves in their new country.

**PASSOVER TEACUP**
Poland, *c.*1880
Ceramic
80 x 82 mm
Cup decorated with swirling ridges and with Hebrew words in gold lettering, reading 'For the Festival of Passover'. The service would have been used only during Passover, when eating bread or other leavened products is forbidden. Jews traditionally use separate crockery and utensils for cooking and eating during the festival, to ensure that they have not been used for proscribed food.
1998.33.1

# FROM EAST TO WEST

Another important group of migrants to Britain came from the former Ottoman Empire. Most of the Jewish population there had come from Spain and Portugal after the expulsions of 1492 and 1495, although the community could trace its roots back to Classical times. There were substantial numbers of Jewish people in Salonika, Baghdad, Izmir and elsewhere in Ottoman territories before 1914, but the First World War and the Balkan Wars led to the break up of the empire, and thousands of Sephardi Jews fled, some of them to England. They joined the small communities of their compatriots already present in London and Manchester. The Manchester cotton trade had drawn immigrants from the Ottoman Empire from the mid-nineteenth century onwards, and by 1872 there were thirty-five families living there, while small numbers of carpet dealers from Constantinople, Salonika and Smyrna had remained in London following the Franco-British Exhibition of 1908.

The Jewish community of Baghdad was of ancient origin, and by the time Iraq was created under British mandate after the First World War, a quarter of the city's population was Jewish. However, with the rise of anti-Semitic violence in Iraq during the Second World War, large numbers of Jews left the country. Many went to India, where there was already a community of Jews of Middle Eastern origin, who had originally travelled east to establish trading links. Notable among those already in India were members of the powerful Sassoon family, who were well integrated into Anglo-Indian society. The Bombay branch of their family business had been set up in 1832 by David Sassoon, who is pictured in traditional dress in an engraving from the Alfred Rubens Collection (AR 2214). Some Baghdadi Jews went directly to England, where another branch of the Sassoon family lived, and where Baghdadi

*Top right:*
**THE DANGOOR FAMILY**
Baghdad, 1910
Photograph
The family of Chief Rabbi Hakham Ezra Dangoor in Baghdad. Left to right: grand-daughter Muzli, grandson Saleh Basri, daughter Farha Shaoul Basri, Hakham Dangoor and his wife, Habiba.
732.21

*Right:*
***THE LATE DAVID SASSOON ESQRE.***
Place of origin unknown, nineteenth century
Steel engraving
213 x 158 mm
Portrait of David Sassoon (1792–1864), Baghdadi-Indian merchant, banker and philanthropist, wearing a turban and Eastern dress.
AR 2214

*Above:*
**BODICE**
Calcutta, mid-nineteenth to
early twentieth century
Brocade, silk thread
Red and gold lady's bodice in
the Baghdadi-Indian style. This
bodice belonged to a woman
from Aleppo, Syria, who
emigrated to Calcutta in the
nineteenth century.
C 2003.5.1

*Right:*
**MAN'S STRIPED ROBE**
Calcutta, mid-nineteenth to
early twentieth century
Silk
Red and green striped robe in
the Baghdadi-Indian style. This
robe belonged to a man from
Aleppo, Syria, who emigrated to
Calcutta in the nineteenth
century.
C 2003.5.10

businessmen had been established in Manchester since the 1880s. Baghdadi and other Jews from India began to come to Britain in the late 1850s, continuing to arrive from Bombay and Calcutta until 1939. The family who owned a spectacular robe (C 2003.5.10) and bodice (C 2003.5.1), along with many other gorgeously decorated items of clothing in the traditional Baghdadi–Indian style, had come originally from Syria, before moving first to Calcutta and later to England.

When India was granted independence in 1947, and the State of Israel was created in the following year, an exodus of Indian Jews began. Although there was no history of anti-Semitism in India, many Jews left in the 1950s and 1960s. After the departure of the British, some Jews were concerned about their situation, while others wished to make a new life in Israel. As well as Baghdadis, these emigrants included Cochin Jews from southern India, and also Bene Israel, India's most numerous Jewish community, from the west of the country. Many came to London, and a photograph in the Jewish Museum's collection (1199-A.3) shows an Indian woman and girl outside the Jews' Temporary Shelter in 1965, a year in which the shelter helped people from Tunisia, Aden and Cyprus, as well as India and Pakistan.

*Left:*
**THE ABRAHAMS FAMILY**
Bombay Photographic Company, Bombay, *c.*1910–14
Photograph
This studio portrait of the Abrahams family, members of the Bene Israel community, shows Menachem (born 1896), Joseph and Rahama, with Joseph's daughters Shegulah and Esther. Menachem served in the British Army during the First World War, and his descendants moved to London in the 1960s.
1340.1

*Right:*
**JEWS' TEMPORARY SHELTER**
London, 1965
Photograph
Jewish immigrants from India outside the Jews' Temporary Shelter, Mansell Street, London. From the Jews' Temporary Shelter annual report for 1965. In that year the shelter assisted immigrants from India, Pakistan, Tunisia, Aden and Cyprus.
1199-A.3

*Left:*
**SPICE TOWER**
Persia, nineteenth century
Silver
190 mm high
The octagonal foot, body and
steeple of this spice tower are
chased with formal foliage
designs.
JM 444

*Opposite:*
***RIMMONIM***
Persia (or Afghanistan?),
late seventeenth century
Silver-gilt, turquoise
320 x 105 mm
Silver-gilt *rimmonim* with
turquoise tips.
C 2001.5.3

The Jewish community of Iran, like that of Iraq, was established during the Babylonian exile in the sixth century BCE. Under Islamic rule the Jews worked as craftspeople, shopkeepers, merchants and bankers. By the seventeenth century the community reached a peak of about 30,000, with major centres in Tehran, Isfahan and Hamadan, reputed to be the birthplace of Esther and Mordechai. In the mid-eighteenth century some Jews were forcibly transferred to Mashad, where they suffered recurrent waves of persecution and were forced to practise their religion in secret. In the early twentieth century many Jews left Mashad for Tehran and other cities, although many other Persian Jews remained scattered in rural areas, often working as carpet weavers like their Muslim neighbours.

Increasing secularisation and westernisation in the 1920s brought more opportunities for Jews to study and work abroad. During this period Mashadi fur and carpet traders emigrated to London. With the fall of the Shah and the Islamic Revolution of 1979, the situation of minorities in Iran deteriorated, and Jewish emigration from Tehran and other major cities escalated. While the majority have settled in Israel, New York or Los Angeles, a significant number of Iranian Jews have made their homes in London and Manchester.

Jewish ceremonial art of the region had a distinctively Middle Eastern style, as exemplified by a pair of silver-gilt *rimmonim* tipped with turquoise (C 2001.5.3).

# Central Europe

The Jews of Central Europe differed in many ways from those living further east and perhaps appeared more familiar to the British. Although they were Ashkenazim, and often the descendants of migrants from Eastern Europe, by the late nineteenth century they had developed a much less traditionalist outlook. They spoke German or Hungarian rather than Yiddish, and increasingly dressed in a Western manner. They were also influenced by the surrounding cultural traditions. The finely made Hungarian bridal head-cover (C 1975.7.14.1) was embroidered by Eugenie Ullman in 1890 for her own wedding, and brought to England by her family. Its delicately worked floral pattern is characteristic of the decorative embroidery found on folk costume from Central and Eastern Europe.

Their generally high level of assimilation increased the terrible shock felt by these communities at the persecution they faced when the Nazis' power spread across Europe. By 1939 half of Germany's 600,000 Jews had left the country; of these, more than 60,000 came to Britain. Again, they often brought with them objects of religious significance, such as a spice tower brought from Pless in 1939 (C 1982.7.13.2). Despite its relatively recent manufacture, this was valued as a family heirloom, carrying associations of memory and continuity as well as religious tradition. More refugees from occupied Europe arrived during the next few years; some took tortuous routes, such as the family who carried their possessions, including a silk *kippah* (1987.114, see p.173), with them from Breslau to Shanghai and on from there to England. It is small, easily portable and personally important objects such as these which typify the possessions brought by immigrants to their new homes, especially when they have been forced to leave at short notice.

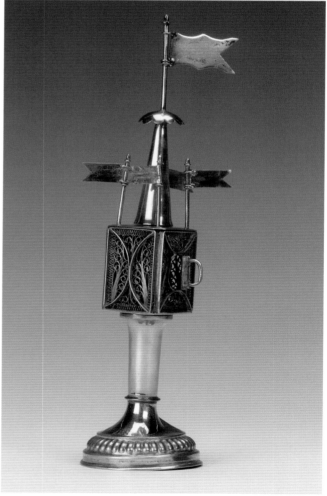

*Top right:*
**BRIDE'S EMBROIDERED HEAD-COVER**
Eugenie Ullman, Hungary, 1890
Silk, lace
762 x 623 mm
Cream-coloured kerchief embroidered with silver thread in a floral design, with hand-made lace edging. Made by the bride for her own wedding.
C 1975.7.14.1

*Right:*
**SPICE BOX**
Germany, *c*.1900
Silver
200 mm high
Spice tower with round base and rectangular filigree tower with an oval door. Four flags on the tower, and a fifth flag on the finial. It belonged to Herta Reece's family, who lived in Pless (now in Poland). Mrs Reece brought it with her when she came to Britain in 1939.
C 1982.7.13.2

# After 1948

The establishment of the State of Israel in 1948 had a major impact on the distribution of Jewish communities across the post-war world. While large-scale immigration to Israel took place from many countries, it also sparked various demonstrations of anti-Jewish feeling, particularly in Arab lands, and the situation of Jews in those regions deteriorated markedly. As a result, in the years that followed, Jews left areas such as Yemen, Aden, Iran, Iraq, Afghanistan, India and North Africa, often in very difficult circumstances. While most went to Israel, some came to Britain.

The Yemeni community was an extremely ancient one, established in the first century BCE. They had absorbed elements of the local culture – an elaborate necklace in the Museum's collection (C 1978.1.5.1a) carries a biblical quotation in Hebrew which is written in Persian script, and the overall form of the necklace is that of a traditional *m'anakeh*, worn by Yemeni married women.

**NECKLACE**
Yemen (or Persian Gulf?), late nineteenth century
Silver-gilt
453 mm long
Bead necklace with triangular end-pieces. Decorated on one side with granulation and filigree, and with a biblical quotation in Hebrew written in Persian script on the other. There are seven strands to the necklace, with alternating beads either granulated and five-sided or diamond-shaped and multi-faceted.
C 1978.1.5.1a

*Above:*

**DEMOISELLE JUIVE D'ALGER ('JEWISH
YOUNG LADY OF ALGIERS')**

Wood engraving after an original by
Duverger, France, 1843-44
143 x 70 mm
Illustration of a young woman in
traditional Algerian-Jewish costume.
AR 46

*Opposite:*

**BEACH PICNIC
AT LITTLE ADEN**

Aden, *c.*1950–60
Photograph
634.9

*Left:*

**RIMMON**

Tunisia, probably seventeenth or
eighteenth century
Wood
350 mm high
One of a pair of wooden *rimmonim* with
two tiers of carved ornamentation,
made up of recesses separated by leaves.
Baluster handles. Painted in green with
gilt on the leaves, and recesses in red.
JM 101 & JM 101a

The neighbouring Jewish community of Aden had been significant in the twelfth century, and, following a decline until the nineteenth century, was revitalised in 1869 by the opening of the Suez Canal, which attracted immigrants from places such as Egypt, India and Turkey. By the 1930s some 8,000 Jews lived in Aden, a society very different from others in the Persian Gulf by virtue of its status as a British Crown Colony and free port. The modern character of the community is illustrated by a photograph from the Museum's archives showing a picnic on the beach at Little Aden in the 1950s (634.9), in which the family sit on deckchairs wearing Western dress. The Six Day War of 1967, combined with anti-British riots in the same year, signalled the end for the last Jewish families in Aden, who were forced to flee for their lives. There is now a vibrant Adeni community in London, including some who moved on to Britain from Israel.

In North Africa Jewish communities had lived peacefully as a religious and national minority among the ruling Arabs from the seventh century until the mid-twentieth century. Despite the large numbers of immigrants from Spain and Portugal in the late fifteenth century, the Ladino language never took over from Judeo-Arabic, and the Sephardim were effectively assimilated into the local Jewish majority. The ceremonial art of the region was likewise influenced by local styles, as illustrated by a pair of simple carved and painted wooden *rimmonim* (JM 101). Small numbers of Jews came to England from Morocco and elsewhere in North Africa to engage in the textile trade in the eighteenth and nineteenth centuries, integrating with the Sephardi communities of London and Manchester. More arrived in the period after 1947, as their situation at home deteriorated. In the 1980s a Moroccan synagogue was established in London.

A further political event that precipitated large-scale Jewish immigration to Britain was the Suez crisis of 1956, after which thousands of Jews fled from Cairo and Alexandria. One of these Egyptian Jews brought to England a striking object, now in the Museum: an intricately decorated Torah case, with inlays in various woods, mother-of-pearl and ivory (C 1980.3.10.1). This case was originally presented to the Alexandria synagogue by the Rolo family, and the influences on its design are clear in the geometric pattern of the inlay work, reminiscent of Islamic tile patterns.

These successive phases of immigration to Britain, mostly produced by catastrophic events overtaking various Jewish communities across the world, have created a Jewish community varied in roots and cultural backgrounds. This is evident from the physical reminders of their heritage brought to Britain from around the world; the clothes, religious artefacts, photographs and other objects are characteristic of the widely divergent societies where Jewish people have lived over the centuries, ranging across Europe, Asia and North Africa. These objects embody the diversity of the community whose stories the Jewish Museum seeks to tell.

*Opposite:*
**TORAH CASE**
Cairo, late nineteenth to early twentieth century
Wood, mother-of-pearl, ivory
442 x 279 mm
Torah scroll and round wooden case of Eastern type. The case has inlaid decoration in various woods, mother-of-pearl and ivory. Inscription in Hebrew inlaid in mother-of-pearl.
C 1980.3.10.1

*Below:*
***HANUKAH* LAMP**
Tunisia (or possibly Balkans or Turkey?), *c.*1800
Silver, glass
392 x 581 mm
Shaped backplate with pierced arcaded gallery or loggia. Base plate pierced to take pendant glass burners. Beadle light held by balcony, above Hebrew inscription flanked by cypress trees. Engraved border of vines.
JM 265

# GLOSSARY

**Amidah**  'Standing'; the standing prayer, an important component of every service.

**Arba kanfot**  'Four corners'; fringed undergarment worn by observant Jewish men.

**Ashkenazim**  'People from Germany'; Jews of Central and East European origin.

**Ba'al Shem**  'Master of the Name'; a title given to someone who could work miracles by use of the 'Holy Names' of God.

**Barmitzvah**  'Son of Commandment'; a boy's coming of age at thirteen years old, usually marked by a synagogue ceremony and a family celebration.

**Batmitzvah**  'Daughter of Commandment'; a girl's coming of age at twelve years old, marked in different ways by different communities.

**Bimah**  Raised platform in a synagogue, from which the Torah is read.

**Edot Hamizrach**  Jews of Eastern origin, often colloquially referred to as Sephardim.

**Etrog**  Citrus fruit used during the festival of *Sukkot* ('Tabernacles').

**Gemara**  Commentary on the *Mishnah*; part of the Talmud.

**Haftarah**  'Completion'; passages from Prophets read in the synagogue, linked to weekly Torah readings.

**Haggadah**  'Telling'; book read at *Pesach* (Passover) telling the story of the Exodus from Egypt (plural *Haggadot*).

**Halachah**  'The Way'; the ongoing process of Jewish law-making, encompassing all aspects of life.

**Hallah**  Rich bread, usually plaited, eaten on the Sabbath and during festivals.

**Hamsa**  Amulet in the shape of a hand.

**Hanukah**  'Dedication'; festival of lights celebrating the re-dedication of the Temple following the Maccabean victory over the Greeks.

**Havdalah**  'Distinction'; ceremony marking the conclusion of *Shabbat*.

**Hazan**  Leader of reading, singing and chanting in some synagogue services.

**Hevra**  Small synagogue (plural *hevrot*).

**Hevra kadisha**  'Holy fellowship', responsible for preparing the bodies of the deceased for burial.

**Hiddur mitzvah**  'Beautification of the commandment'; the principle that the service of the Lord should be performed using beautiful objects

**Huppah**  Canopy under which a bride and groom stand during their wedding ceremony.

**Kabbalah**  Form of Jewish mysticism.

**Kashrut**  Laws relating to keeping a *kosher* diet.

**Ketubah**  Contract defining rights and obligations within Jewish marriage (plural *ketubot*).

**Kiddush**  'Holy'; a prayer sanctifying Shabbat and festival days, usually recited over wine.

Kindertransport  Evacuation of Jewish children from Germany, Austria and Czechoslovakia to Britain before the Second World War.

**Kippah**  Head-covering worn by observant Jewish men during prayers and Torah study, and by some at all times (plural *kippot*).

**Kosher**  'Fit, proper'; foods permitted by Jewish dietary laws.

Ladino  Language derived from Spanish and Hebrew, historically spoken by Sephardim.

**Lulav**  Branches of palm, myrtle and willow used on *Sukkot* ('Tabernacles').

**Ma'asim tovim**  Good deeds; includes both ethical and moral *mitzvot*.

**Magen David**  'Shield of David', commonly called 'Star of David'.

**Matzah**  Flat cracker-like bread eaten at *Pesach*.

**Megillah**  Book of Esther, read on *Purim*.

**Menorah**  Seven-branched candelabrum which was lit daily in the Temple.

**Mezuzah**  Scroll fixed to the doorposts of Jewish homes, containing a section from the *Shema*; often enclosed in a decorative case (plural *mezuzot*).

Midrash  A genre of rabbinic literature comprising homilies, stories and legends.

**Mishnah**  First transcription of Jewish oral law, codified around 200 CE; part of the Talmud.

**Mitzvah**  'Commandment'; one of the 613 commandments of the Torah; commonly used to describe good deeds (plural *mitzvot*).

**Mizrach**  Wall plaque showing the direction of prayer.

**Mohel**  Person trained to perform circumcisions (plural *mohelim*).

| | |
|---|---|
| *Ner tamid* | 'Continual light' placed over the ark in synagogues as a symbol of the Temple *Menorah*. |
| *Omer* | Period of seven weeks between *Pesach* and *Shavuot*. |
| Pale of Settlement | An area within the borders of Tsarist Russia, between the Baltic and the Black Sea, where Jews were permitted to live by law. |
| *Pesach* | Passover, the festival commemorating the Exodus from Egypt. |
| *Pogrom* | Organised attack on Jews, especially frequent in nineteenth- and early twentieth-century Eastern Europe. |
| *Purim* | Festival commemorating the rescue of Persian Jews, as told in the Book of Esther. |
| Rabbi | An ordained Jewish teacher, generally the religious leader of a Jewish community. |
| Rashi | Rabbi Shlomo ben Yitzhak (1040-1105), a French rabbinical scholar. |
| *Rimmonim* | 'Pomegranates'; finials placed on top of Torah scrolls. |
| *Rosh Hashanah* | 'Head of the Year'; Jewish New Year. |
| *Sandak* | The man who holds the baby during the circumcision ceremony, a role generally granted as an honour. |
| *Seder* | 'Order'; ceremonial meal during *Pesach*, at which the Exodus from Egypt is recounted using the *Haggadah*. |
| Sephardim | Jews of Spanish or Portuguese origin; also commonly used to refer to those of southern European, North African or Eastern origin (including *Edot Hamizrach*). |
| *Shabbat* | The Jewish Sabbath, commencing at sunset on Friday and ending at nightfall on Saturday. |
| *Shaddai* | 'Almighty'; a name of God, also used to describe amulets which feature that name. |
| *Shavuot* | 'Weeks'; festival of Pentecost, celebrating the divine revelation of the giving of the Torah. |
| *Shechita* | Method of ritual slaughter prescribed by *kashrut* laws. |
| *Sheitel* | Wig worn by very observant Jewish women following marriage, to cover their hair as an expression of modesty. |
| *Shema* | Important Jewish prayer affirming the belief in one God. |
| *Shochet* | Ritual butcher, responsible for slaughtering animals. |
| *Shofar* | Ram's horn blown during *Rosh Hashanah* and *Yom Kippur*. |
| *Simchat Torah* | 'Rejoicing of the Law'; festival celebrating the completion of the cycle of the weekly Torah reading. |
| *Sukkah* | 'Tabernacle'; a temporary dwelling used during *Sukkot*. |
| *Sukkot* | 'Tabernacles'; autumn harvest festival and remembrance of the forty years of wandering in the wilderness after the Exodus from Egypt. |
| Synagogue | Place of Jewish public prayer, study and assembly. |
| *Tallit* | Four-cornered prayer shawl with fringes. |
| Talmud | Book comprising the transcription of Jewish oral law (*Mishnah*) and commentaries on that law (*Gemara*). |
| *Tebah* | Sephardi term for the synagogue reading desk, equivalent to '*bimah*'. |
| *Tedeschi* | Italian name for Ashkenazi Jews, particularly those from Germany. |
| *Tefillin* | Phylacteries; small boxes containing passages from the Torah, strapped onto the forehead and arm of observant Jewish men for morning prayers. |
| *Tik* | Torah case, used in Eastern communities instead of a Torah mantle. |
| Torah | 'Law, teaching'; the Five Books of Moses; also used to refer to Jewish law in general. |
| *Tzedakah* | 'Righteousness'; an act of charity. |
| *Tzitzit* | Fringes on the corners of the *tallit*; also commonly refers to the *arba kanfot*. |
| *Yad* | 'Hand'; hand-shaped pointer used in reading the Torah scroll. |
| *Yahrzeit* | 'Year-time'; anniversary of a death. |
| Yiddish | Language derived from Hebrew and German, used predominantly by Ashkenazim. |
| *Yom Kippur* | Day of Atonement, day of prayer and fasting ten days after *Rosh Hashanah*. |
| Zionism | Political movement advocating the return of Jewish people to the land of Israel. |

# INDEX

marriage contracts *see ketubah*
medieval Jewish community 21
*Megillah* (Esther scroll) 62–3, 144–5
*memento mori* paintings 116–17
Menasseh ben Israel, Rabbi 22
Mendoza, Daniel 23, 119, 124–5, *126*, 127
*mezuzah* 51, 52, *53*, *104*
migrants *see immigrants*
military service 38, 167
*mitzvot* (commandments) 51, 52
*mizrach* 33, 41, *42*, *94*, 95
*mohel* books 107
Montagu, Samuel 148
Montefiore, Sir Moses 28

naturalisation 30–1, 120
Netherlands 22, 76–7, 116
Newton, Richard 119, *122*, 128, *129*
North Africa, migration from 185–7

Oliveyra, Abraham de 56, 79–80
*Omer* calendars 66, 142–3
Ottoman Empire 98, 177

Passover *see Pesach*
pedlars 24, 122–3, 125
Perkoff, Isaac *149*, *150*
*Pesach* (Passover) 65–6
    cushion *92*, 93
    *Haggadah* 65, 133, 134, 136, 140–1
plates *34*, *54*, *65*, 66, *111*
*pogroms* 33, 147
pointer, Torah (*yad*) 50
political life 30–1, 100
prayer books *51*, *71*, 135–9
    *Haggadah* 65, 133, 134, 136, 140–1
prayer/prayer artefacts 51–3, 95, 97
the press 154
printed books 133–4
prints 14, 118–31
*Purim* 62
*Purim* scrolls 62–3, 133, 144–5

Ramberg, J. H. 124, 128
'racial' caricature 124–5, 131
readmission by Oliver Cromwell 22, *119*, 120, 172
Reform Judaism 28
refugees from Nazism 37–8, 158–71, 182
*rimmonim* 46, *47*, 77, 79–80, 81, 180, *184*, 185
rings,
    marriage 70, 75, 112, *113*

medieval signet ring *21*
rites of passage 68–72, 103–17
*Rosh Hashanah* (New Year) 57
Rothschild, Lionel de 30
Rothschild, Nathan Mayer 24, 125
Rowlandson, Thomas 119, *122*, 123, 124

the Sabbath (*Shabbat*) 54–6
Salomons, Sir David 30, *32*, 92
Sassoon family 177
satirical prints *30*, *31*, 119, 120–31
Schlesinger, Dr Bernard 160
schools and schooling *29*, 156, 159, 160
scribe-artists 136–8, 140, 141
scrolls,
    artefacts for 46–50, 79–81
    *Megillah* 62–3, 144–5
    *Omer* calendars 66, 142–3
    *Purim* scrolls 62–3, 133, 144–5
    *see also* binders; breast plates; cases;
        crowns; mantles; pointers; Torah
Second World War and after 166–71
*Seder* 65–6
Sephardi community 21, 23, 42, 173, 177, 185
Sephardi square script 142
*Shaddai* 105
*Shavuot* (Pentecost) 66
*Shema* 51–2
*shofar* 57
Shuster, Dora *150*
silversmiths 56, 77, 79, 80, 81
silver,
    for daily religious life *51*, 54–6, 83–5
    festival artefacts *59*, *60*, *63*, 82
    for life cycle rituals *68*, 70, *71*, 72,
        87, *103*, *104*, 105
    for secular use 75–6, *86–9*
    synagogue/ceremonial use *14*
    Torah ornaments 46, *47*, *49–50*, 75,
        77–81
*Simchat Torah* festival 58
Sopher, Abraham 141
Spackman, William 79
Stern, Erhard (Edward) 167
souvenirs, textiles as 97–8
spice containers 54, *55*, 83–5, *180*, 182
*Sukkot* (Tabernacles) 58
synagogues 14, 23, *26*, 27, 28, *39*, 41–50, 82, 88, 148

tailoring trade *17*, 151–2
*tallit* 52
    bags *97*

Talmud, the 50
*tefillin* cases and bags 51, 97
textiles,
    domestic and personal 93–6, 103, *105*
    secular uses 98, 100–1
    in the synagogue 91–2
    *see also* ark curtains; binders; clothes;
        mantles; *mizrach*
Thau, Martin 166
theatre, Yiddish 154
*tik* (Torah case) 46, *49*, 186
Torah, 50
    artefacts for 46–50, 77, 79–81
    *see also* binders; breast plates; cases;
        crowns; illustration; mantles;
        pointers; scrolls
trades 16–17, *34*, *147*, 151–3
    in early communities 21, 23
trade unions 100, 152
Tuchmann, Bernhard 167
*tzedakah* 73
*tzitzit* 51, 52

weddings *see marriage*
Weizmann, Chaim 36
*wimpel* (or *mappah*) 68, 107–8
woodwork, synagogue items *41*, 44, *49*
Workers' Circle 154

*yad see pointer*
*yahrzeit* 72, 115
Yemen 183
Yiddish language 173
Yiddish theatre *see theatre, Yiddish*
*Yom Kippur* (Day of Atonement) 57, *98*

Zangwill, Israel 34
Zionism 34, 36

© Scala Publishers Ltd, 2006
© Text and images The Jewish Museum, London 2006

First published in 2006 by
Scala Publishers Ltd
Northburgh House
10 Northburgh Street
London EC1V 0AT

ISBN 1 85759 457 6 (hardback); ISBN 1 85759 413 4 (paperback)

Editors: Rickie Burman, Jennifer Marin and Lily Steadman
Photography: Ian Lillicrapp and Jan Lawrie
Project Editor: Esme West
Designer: Janet James
Printed and bound in Italy

10 9 8 7 6 5 4 3 2 1

The following illustrations are licensed for reproduction:
Louis XIV silver dressing-table service (p. 76) © The Devonshire Collection,
Chatsworth. Reproduced by permission of the Chatsworth Settlement
Trustees.
Pair of George III silver *rimmonim* (p. 80) © Christie's Images Ltd (1995)
George II silver-gilt ewer and basin (p. 86) © Christie's Images Ltd
*Moses Chusing his Cook* (p. 128) courtesy of The Library of The Jewish
Theological Seminary, New York
Theatre posters from the Grand Palais Collection (endpapers and p.155)
by permission of Mr Basil Greenby

British Library Cataloguing in Publication Data. A catalogue record for this
book is available from the British Library.

*Front cover:*
Nineteenth-century English amulet and pointer (see p. 69)

*Back cover:*
Banner of the London Jewish Bakers' Union, 1920s (see p. 101)

*Cover flaps:*
*Etrog* box by Milla Tanya Griebel, England, 2001 (see p. 59)
Baking tools from Goldring's Bakery, London, *c.*1935–85 (see p. 146)

*Frontispiece:*
Eighteenth-century miniature Torah scroll, probably English
Pouch of documents carried by Richard Kaufmann on the Kindertransport, 1939
(see p. 164)

*Dedication:*
*Procession of the Law,* by Solomon Alexander Hart RA, *c.*1845–50 (see p. 58)
Nineteenth-century Bohemian glass Cup of Elijah (see p. 64)

*Contents page:*
Seventeenth-century glass Sabbath lamp (see p. 42)

*Acknowledgements page:*
Eighteenth-century spice tower, Germany or Eastern Europe (see p. 85)